AF424108

we are all connected.
we are living our own
story where each one
of us is someone within
it. hidden or seen, we all
are a part of something
bigger than what we see.

-karnes-

SONDER

Chapter I

-INTRO TO SELF-

There is a place where lovers go, where the sane find peace in the beginning of things more so than the ending of it all. I have never been sane enough to understand the monotony this place places upon its own kind. I have always been a little all over the place when it comes to my thoughts and the origin of my center. Stories are told daily by those strange enough to hear them when the world goes silent. In the harbor of my soul you will find boats overturned and capsized by the waves of change and the inevitably life sets us on fire with. You will find humans walking in all directions based on feeling and not because they are told where to go. There is a needed chaos I must have in my life to restore the normalcy I oftentimes go without. We are at best, an awakening to some, and at worst, death by a thousand goodbyes because we simply cannot for the life of us figure out what we want, so we continue going back to the source of our happiness regardless of fate. There will be more who fall victim to this saga. Unfortunately for them, they have no idea it will be them until it is too late and everyone has a finger pointing at them, laughing and smirking as they walk by knowing what is in store for them. Life has a goddamn cruelty to it that no one can simply prepare for. They must live it to see for themselves just how fucked it all can be. I have always been a positive person. A half-cup full kind of guy. Growing up, I needed there to be room for error so I could fill in the missing parts with what I had to have at that time. Some of the time it was drugs, other times it was just complete silence to counteract the dead noise in my head and life. We meet people throughout our lives who are struggling with everything. Struggling with words to find, love to keep, and a sickness when they thought it was beaten. Millions of us walk around with mountains invading our space that feel like they will never stop growing. They feel like lessons we fucking swear we have learned from, yet they only keep us from the sun we so desperately are in need of. Light comes in many forms. It can be a smile. It can be a holding hand. It can be someone who only wishes to listen to our madness. It can be a sunny day after being covered in clouds and rain for years, hoping to break away from the darkness. We are not what we think, but we are what we do when all that is left is to chase after what we love. After it has been taken away or be it something we have lost along the way. I am still in search of peace, and maybe it exists in the next day. There is not an exact science as to how we are supposed to live our lives and it is why we all go insane for things we can never have. We feel as if we are entitled to everything that comes our way. The only thing we are entitled to is the pursuit of complete freedom and knowing death sleeps next to our dreams, teasing it with a promise to always be there. It is the most fucked up tease of all time, because it all ends. We end. Our love ends. Our breath becomes another inhale for someone else to take. Everything meaningful and beautiful wilts and is destroyed by the aftermath. At least for a little while until our feet regrow themselves and find footing that can sustain day a human not meant or created to stand still. Promises of any type are a mixed bag. Some believe in everything, while others believe in nothing, and that is when all hell can break loose. That is when our generational pull is weakened. Do not become lost to the flame because you are shivering and in need of warmth. Walk amongst the trees and allow them to tell you a story of how they have survived all this time while we have continually taken from them and their families. There is strength in numbers, but there is also strength in one. Being alone can feel like the worst life ever meant to be associated with who you are, but imagine being with someone who you think loves you, only to feel the cold night pressed against you instead of a body. Imagine being told of all the love you ever wanted was in someone who was unwilling to give you what you have always been able to give to others. We are constantly made to believe in something that may or may not exist based on keeping up with the status quo and not feeling left out of something that we could have as well.

The truth is, some are meant for a life forever filled love and never knowing what being alone feels like. The rest of us keep to our side, hoping whatever god we pray to sends us resilience to make it through another winter striking our own heart against a stone left by the last one who used it to do the same just for a chance to feel something warm, to feel something instead of being numbed by our ideals and logic taught to us long before we understood our own language. Life presents itself to us all differently and in certain times of our lives, it can feel like we are attending our own funeral.   One of which we can see it all being played out and how gracious everyone is and was to have known us. It is in between living and dying we are born. We are brought into this world to die unfortunately. We go without a say as to how it is we do, but we certainly have a fucking say in how we live it. we will arrive where we are needed, in all ways. Be brave in the chase and never forget those before you who never got a chance to see the tomorrow you are living today. Being taught and raised by an alcoholic mother, I learned first hand how it   is to feel unwanted and neglected by someone you love. Some relationships take a while until they hit that part head on and it is such a fucking blow to the soul to know they never loved you as much as they lead you to believe. It is a feeling I hope no one ever has to feel, much less feel when they are still a young kid developing tools for the life ahead of them. It makes some of us cold and we end up abandoning any hope of ever making it to who we wanted to be. Struggle creates immense adversity, but it can also create and mend the most broken of humans into a giver of love unknown to those who never went through or experienced hard times. Who never experienced someone disowning them at a young age or what they offered. My mother did her best considering the circumstances, but being that young, it takes decades to clean and rinse it from your life so you don't give it to anyone else. For all of the bullshit I was made to live in, I am thankful for the lessons and the boy I was for not completely giving up and saying fuck it all. I started smoking at a young age to camouflage my pain. I was eleven when I started. I still remember finding the pack of Harley Davidson's in the garage bathroom underneath a few folded up shirts, then I was hooked. Drinking came natural to me since I had seen it my whole life. I knew how much it would take to forget the day and there was never enough to do so. But i kept at it until I was throwing up every word ever said to me. Until every feeling of hatred and ache left my body. I heaved up memories and bones of old, probably not even mine, but it all came up each time I drank. I became an alcoholic by the time I was a teenager. Dealing with inside issues, you must confront it before it becomes a disease. Before it deteriorates who you are at your core. Do not become inhumane simply based on your childhood or because someone mistreated you years ago. We must not allow our anger to fester and become an asylum for our human side. We must not allow angst to hold our love hostage. Many go to sea thinking they will return, but a piece always dies out there we will never get back. We have the power to change, to help others change themselves if they are ready for it. I learned we cannot help and treat those who aren't ready for it. It is our duty to maintain a positive outlook and trust in the process of becoming. We cannot have others be the protectors of what we carry. We must carry it on our own to wherever the journey takes us. You are not cursed because you feel too much. You are not cursed because you love too much. It is only a disservice if you wish to feel and remain in that mindset. Not enough people get the chance or opportunity to experience it for themselves. They have no idea how beautiful it is to be in touch with a universe, with a world, with another avenue of life and love. Being an empath has been a challenge for me. Probably one of the most daunting things I have ever had to control or at least attempt to in all of my years of breathing on this planet. Five years ago, I finally understood what it meant and why I did all the drugs and drank all the alcohol to keep from feeling all the energy. Writing and working out has been the saving grace for me. Reconnecting with my inner-child and grief matured me. which brought on the help I truly needed from myself. I also learned how to channel it in a more complete approach. It took me years to get here to this point, to this feeling of nirvana so to speak. Though I am still a beginner and novice at best, I have taken the right steps to ensure a longer life of bliss for me and whomever wishes to be a part of my path. My energy never mixed well with chaos, but now I am living proof you can be all kinds of chaotic and still function within the confines of your soul and this realm. Every day I am more incessantly aware of what is needed of me and from me. Each day you have a choice to carry or take what you need along your way to create what is in your heart. We must remember our lives are all connected in some way. We are all walking together. Maybe not hand in hand, but in spirit. Maybe we didn't come from the same place, but we will all end up going out the same way. Each breath is a goddamn gift. It is an extension of who we are. It is derived from our ancestral tenets. It is a living thing just as we are. It is capable of changing the course of someone's life. It is and will remain the cornerstone of how we get to where we are ultimately needed. Venturing through all obstacles, we are the ship, waves, and compass of each passing entity that comes into contact with who we are and where we have been. Our bodies were made to withstand anything humans could ever do to us. Never let someone break you down so they can build themselves up. Your backbone was not made to be stood upon. It was made to make sure you never needed to lean on anyone else. Though we all need someone or a group to hold us up from time to time, we are not taking from them. They are giving to us. That's the difference many never comprehend. A giving hand can still can make a fist when backed into a corner or provoked. We have the power to maintain any motion we begin and we have to take responsibility for what comes from it. I haven't had many days when I have been able to live my life as I have wanted to the last month or so, but remaining positive despite the chaos going around you is what life is all about. Even if it is demoralizing and soul tearing, it is paramount that we stick to who we are and not allow the outside factors to dictate the inside flow of our energy. I took a two month break from writing this.

I needed to get my life straight and corrected before I continued on writing my story, my lessons, my ever-growing beliefs. I have known of love. I have been a victim to the war it creates within us and around us. I know regardless of what happens to me and my life, my story will survive the bad days. We are created for more than a single purpose. We are meant to be more than just lovers, friends, and acquaintances. There is a deeper meaning to our existence. There is a meaningful way in which we should want to live and breathe amongst each other. Our parallel surfaces are not meant to be simply linear. Meaning our existence is meant to be experienced in the fullest of light. The fullest of colors. The fullest of cardinal directions and sub-directions. This book is a combination of scrambled ideas and thoughts. It is not meant to be followed word for word and page to page. My brain doesn't act that way, nor should it. I am fully aware my style isn't for everyone, but it is for those who think there is more to life. Who think outside of the world in which we live. There is no handbook to life. There is no motivational quote that can save you from the end. There is no motivational speaker that can get you off your ass and keep you off your ass until you feel better about yourself and who you are. We are all trying to find our way. We are all trying to leave our mark or some kind of mark somewhere in this tiny speck of a place spit out by the universe and called earth. This is not a how-to book. This is not a self-help book. This is not anything resembling poetry or prose. It is simply a book I felt compelled to write based on my appetite for continual writing. If I could, I'd write without periods.

Without any type of grammar ridden layout made up of randomly plugging in what the soul thinks of a heart and mind. This is not a manifesto to another galaxy for trying, for loving, or for living. We as humans get too entirely caught up in the next big thing, we forget what we have now. We forget what we have in our fucking grasp. We are always on the lookout for more pictures. More data. More space. More love. More money. More sex. More things to call ours. More and more and more fucking more. Be content for once in your life. Understand all of this will end. All of this you seek will find you before you can find it. Death will not only kiss you, it will sing you the sweetest fucking lullaby to get you to sleep. It will take away the most precious of things you have ever consumed or held or thought about having. I do not want to cheat death. I do not want to cheat love. I just want to live with an honest purpose. In order for me to do that, things will have to be sacrificed. I will have to lock myself away without others to talk to. Without anything more than a single window to know the difference between night and day. Every sunset and sunrise gives me love. It gives me life. It gives me meaning. We awake to a new day and think we will figure it out. We think, "this is the day it all happens." Then we end up drinking the poison and believing all things that are meant to be will find its way to us. But that's not the case. Most of the time, you have to work your ass off and fucking do it yourself. Move by yourself. Rearrange mountains, while climbing each fucking one. We will have to suffer and love by ourselves. We will have to interact with our emotions and feelings. To live, you must gut the stars above and watch our truth spill out. You must take control of any and everything that has a pulse. Depending on others is the quickest way to end up with your heart decapitated and left on a stake for others to see as a warning to stay away from said person. They are probably not worthy of my own to begin with, but I give everyone a benefit of the doubt until they show me otherwise. We are at times probably too gullible for our own good. But if others only knew the fight it took for us to give the hearts we have, the ones they now see, then maybe they'd fall in love again or at least give it a chance for themselves. Maybe there would be a risk large enough or a reason to move on after it all ends the first time. I hope we all get to experience love in some sort of light, but mostly, the kindest of one. It is too precious to fuck around with, yet, we carry it around when we have it as if we will never drop it and break the one thing we had fought an entire life to find. We are destined for our lights to be turned out, for our hearts to stop quivering at the slightest thought of loss. We are not here forever. We are only here for what seems like years upon years, but in the whole scheme of the universe, a few blinks here, a few blinks there, and we are gone, and nothing comes with us. I have read several accounts of those who have been in their eighties and nighties. Someone asked them what they wished they had done differently. They all spoke about doing what they wanted to, but were too timid or afraid to do it because of the fear of what someone else thought. I remember certain excerpts like that more than anything else I've ever read. The regrets of those who've left before making it a full life.

The memory of not doing what you wanted when you were able and wanted to. I think we owe it to ourselves to give our best effort at whatever it is, whenever it appears for us. Don't hold back because you fear judgment of someone else. If we simply feared the loss of not having it to remember, we wouldn't give our worries the time of day. Fear the life it could have brought to you if you had it. Desperation and fear are two of the most world renown motivators. I hope it never comes to either in order for you to feel free for the first time. I hope it doesn't come to that to make you feel as though it is your final chance. Be limitless in every aspect of life. Once we have what we think we need, complacency may visit you. Do not allow it anywhere near you. It is the reaper of all things beautiful and full of life. Do not allow anyone to ever go without hope.

I strive daily to ensure everyone I meet feels appreciated, because at the end of the day, it is what we all can ask for. Being human is difficult already. Do what you can to make sure it isn't a burden. Do everything you can, while you can, because once you commit to it, all else is up for the world to see. We are simply living and breathing entities, with a mind capable of creating the most amazing and in-depth creations. Once we secure ourselves in our art, everything else that comes after it, is the blessing of light we have fought our entire lives to find. Do what you can with what you have, in art and in life. The only judgment I care about personally, is the way I interact with my art and how it makes me feel. I've lived long enough to know what others think and say can only harm you if you let it into your energy. There are greater losses in life, but this isn't one.

SONDER 2 5

Chapter II

-NEW LIFE-

I haven't written much since I finished the first chapter. A lot of life has happened. A lot of living has taken place. I fell in love again for only the fifth time in my life. Though if I am being honest, falling in love for me is easy when it comes to everything around me. I have been that way since I was a child. The sky, fresh cut grass, ice cream during the summer, swimming in the pool and watching birds and wasps come down to take a drink and cool off. Over the last several years it has been difficult to live appropriately due to all of the uncertainty roaming around these lands. Covid hit just as I got back to Texas to help my father out and try to get him moved out of this house. On top of it all, the world shut down for over three years it felt like. My traveling has been reduced to nothing more than writing about a life I hope I get to live one day.

Gas prices are over four dollars and fifty cents. I traded in my car at the end of last year, thinking I had a reason I needed a bigger vehicle. All I got was a more expensive payment and a larger fuel tank to fill up. I have friends who are spending over two hundred dollars a week on just fuel alone. Inflation hit an all time high last week and there is no end in sight it seems for the middle class and those under the ladder without proper footing for the first rung. Summer is here now with temperatures already surpassing one hundred degrees and well above that with heat indexes applied. I remember there was a time in 2004 when I had my dodge pickup which was a diesel, and it was a dollar eighty-five per gallon. I would bitch and complain about it then, but it didn't impact my daily life as it currently does now. I was just a college kid, working at Kroger, partying with my friends, and eating their food without being able to pay for my own. It was simpler times, with days that lasted only until the night caught up with us when we were fifteen beers deep and enough meth running through me to power me on for another four or five days without needing to spend money on food. I was driving back and forth from my dad's house to College Station more times than not, trying to run the road rugged and leave nothing behind. I eventually left and lost contact with all of my friends in the process. The friendships I had made growing up, well over twenty years with the same group, then it is all gone. I joined the Marine Corps a few years later after walking into a recruiting station and almost joining before I had spoke to my dad about it. He told me to wait a few years because I would more than likely be going to Fullujah and ending up on the front lines there and probably dying. So we thought, especially my dad. After getting out in 2010, I moved back in with my father where I would end up staying for four years before moving to South Texas with him in the process. We moved again in 2017 to a different city, but still on the coast. My father lost his job at the end 2018, and at the end of the year, I moved to Utah after taking a road trip to St. George. It is the lifeblood within me. I was starving for a new element and knew I needed change. I had been living with my father longer in my adult years than in my childhood all put together. I stayed there a year until I came back to help him out financially and make sure he was okay. Being his age, I didn't want him to be alone all the time. I spoke to him at least twice a day while I was there. I knew he was struggling and when I decided to come back, I knew it would help him in a lot of different ways. By then I was covered in tattoos and finally got my sleeves done, along with several other ones. It was my favorite part of every month and such a beautiful therapy for me. The tattoo sessions would go into the three hour mark and my tattoo artist became one of my closest friends there. We talked about everything and he introduced me to all kinds of different music in the process. I was there when his wife died and we talked about that for a few sessions. I got my first tattoo when I was seventeen. My father had to sign a waiver for me to get it. I knew that day tattoos would become a huge part of my life. There was never any pain associated with it. I loved every second of the needle doing its job on me. I could escape for as long as it took and not worry about anything else but being present in that moment. Besides working out, it is the only quiet time I truly have had in my entire life. My brain never shuts off. It goes silent for me just long enough at night to sleep, then it starts back up all over again the next day. The last three years almost since I have been back , I have only been able to get a few of them while maintaining my mental edge as well as my physical awareness for a better lifestyle. This coming October will be my seventh year of sobriety. It is something I never knew I would be able to do after living a life full of drinking heavily always and drugs in my younger days. It took its toll on my body and my life as a whole. I knew I was staring down the barrel of a loaded weapon. I knew my finger was on the trigger the entire time. I knew I was the only one who would be able to release it from my grip.

I did, and now being sober is the most addicting thing I've ever done. Each day is its own and brings its own problems, but I maintain it all by focusing on whatever good is left in my life now. I have lost so much. I have loved even more. Nothing has been easy. Everything comes at a heavier price as you get older. All we can do is hope we are as strong as we believe ourselves to be and carry on through it with love plunging out of our eyes for life. I do not know what will come of all the bad and good I have done in my life. I can only give this day my best effort, my love for the living amongst the dead I carry within. Traveling is in my blood. It has been ever since I could walk and push myself in a baby walker as a youngster. My nickname growing up was, bull. My father gave it to me because I was always on the go and running into things head first. It is an accurate depiction of who I am as a whole. If I am not moving, my mind and soul are. Growing up, I was the protector, nurturer, giver, helper. Being the middle child you pick up on things quicker and they ultimately become a part of you. Those things stay with you your entire life. I have never not been the one who has given more, given all I had to prove a point or to keep something in my life from leaving. Every single thing I have held onto, has my nail markings on it, because I know how precious it is to have something or things you love. When it leaves you, you never get those pieces back. If you're lucky, you may find something similar again, but never the same thing twice. I love, love, but at the end of the day, we have to give ourselves the best life we can. Being selfish has never been associated with me, though at this point in my life, I have finally come to terms with being okay with my own needs. I never want to hurt anyone with how and who I am. I've done that more times than I can count. With the wind at my back, I know the wings I have kept in will finally be able to taste a fresh course, a newly minted rendezvous with the version of myself I never allowed myself to be for the sake of taking care of those I loved. A lot of mistakes have been made. A lot of late night talks with the moon have taken place. I often feel more alone than I really am. I listen to sad songs all the time to keep my edge and a profound writing space uncluttered. I've lived at such a frantic pace my entire life. I do not know if I have it in me to slow down. As long as there is an open road in front of me, driving the speed limit is a slow death. I do take my time when it is called for, when the landscape is something new and new life is outside of the windows. My birthday is coming up in a few months. I'll turn thirty-seven. Any birthday after twenty-one feels odd, almost pointless to point out. I never imagined my life making it this far. In my dreams, I never got this far. So in a lot of ways, I am outliving my sleeping parades, taking in life through writing and a camera lens. This year I will be buying my first camera. It is a lost love of mine. My mother used to have old ones all over the house and inside of closets. I would tinker with them and hope there was still film inside of them. But I wasn't that lucky. I used to pretend there was and spend hours taking photos, never being able to see anything other than what I kept in my memory. Love has turned out to be that for me. Something else I have stored away to remind myself it actually did happen and it was real life at a moment when my reality was far from anything resembling perfect. Realness is what we make it. Sometimes it is created from a childhood we barely survived, but found out how to by simply learning new hiding places and spaces outside of the lines drawn for us to remain safe. I struggle daily with it all. It is a hindering attack set out by my own admission that I am not good enough, or at least, not worthy of having all of the things I do. Beauty has found me every five years or so. The kind you only write about, because if you were to openly accept it, it would gladly take the knife from the counter and direct it towards your back when you weren't looking. I am not saying all beauty is out to kill you, but there is a very good chance it will. I have managed to take in a few thousand sunsets, all from different spots in the world. I wish that were true. I have only seen a few of them in Afghanistan, which happened to be the most memorable. War is never a memory you want to rekindle when the night keeps her darkness on you. I do revert back to the way the sun looked like it was from a different planet as I sat on post, admiring its colors and all the sounds around me. Sometimes there was gunfire and rockets. Other times, there were children rustling through the water and goats being herded to some different location. You never forget the sound of bells the goats would wear, nor do you forget the sounds of RPG's being whizzed by you. I am on a journey of truth in my life and what lies beyond this very point where I find myself currently. Poetry keeps me busy, but a mind like mine, it refuses to keep quiet. I do my best with all of it and tell stories or real life occurrences on here, because it softens the demons I carry. It makes them too heavy to walk around barefoot and breaking what is left of me. I am trying to write at least a few pages a day for this book. I am not even sure what to call this based on the randomness that pops into my mind. I think it is directionless for a reason, since each new day brings a new season with it. A relic of olden times when I thought I was safe inside a home that produced more demons than ghosts themselves. I battle constantly to stay above the water, to remain above ground on my most difficult days. I know I don't speak openly about them, but I think it is for my own good I keep trying to sit with it all and figure out the best way to nurture my soul back to life. it has been a tumultuous last few years for me and millions of others living in this world. A pandemic nearly kept us all in the dark for almost three years. We were cut off from family and friends, from holidays when family is all we really have to show for anything. I may have become hopeless and restless even more than I already was. I remember when it hit me. It was the day Kobe Bryant died in the helicopter crash, along with his little girl and others who were on their way to a basketball game. It was such a shock to my system, I become inundated with feelings and emotions I hadn't felt in fucking years. I was scared and visibly distraught with a terror, knowing if he can die as he did along with those who were with him, this world isn't going to keep any of us safe. My anxiety reared its ugliness again, and I made a choice to get medication for it. It only lasted six months before I stopped taking them. I'd rather live with it all than go around as a zombie and sleeping half the day away. We do what is best for us, even if it means suffering a bit more to remain human. I do my best trying to detach myself, from myself. It is the best way for me to approach anything with an open mind. It is the only way I know how to be who I am. It gives me power over the doubts and fears I once had before giving myself to a feeling or emotion trying to come through. I believe we all have the ability to shape and shift our mindsets when the time calls for us to do so. This book has become more of a journal than a book. Each day I write as long as I can, when I can, and hope something sticks to these pages. Any form of prose has been the easiest for me. I get into this groove, this other-world, and I am free again. I forget what's happening around me and I become as lost as the moon is during the brightest of days. I wish there were easier days for all of us. I wish we weren't made to be broken, and for those who say they are not, I won't ever believe you. This life is too demanding, too visceral for any of us to ever make it out of it without scars designed specifically for us to wear. I have more than enough for those who say they don't have any. Mine are all named and I remember vividly each one as if it were my own child. There have been nights I have stayed awake, wondering if I would ever make it to see the next day. My anxiety is a motherfucker. It leads me to ponder more than I should about shit I shouldn't even give power to. I wasn't always like this. I once could be on a plane without any fears popping into my head. I used to not even think about the things I think about today. I don't know how it changed and rewired who I am. I guess war does change you. Be it overseas or being in love. We tell ourselves nothing is wrong when the entire fucking world around us is going through and beyond the gates of hell. We are warriors, yet, we forget how to raise our swords when it matters most to us. We forget what it takes even though we are bleeding all over this earth to make sure we survive the next place. Never give into the shadows in your mind. The sun never cowers when it sees itself fade. The moon never resists dancing in the middle of the a brand new morning, even though her fight is done for the day. May we all get to a point in our lives when we feel a balance of heart and soul, instead of a teetering of life and death. Our time will come towards the end of a twilight when we are old and gray, remembering every good thing we ever did. The life we have and are living is worth every ounce of sacrifice to ensure our survival of body and mind. Without a proper appreciation for who we are and who we see when the mirror finds us, tells us all we need to know when it comes to discovering what is left for us to do. I have been managing this life of mine without a broken heart for decades it seems, if not longer. I was born with it, shaped by it, and even in an infancy of breathing, I knew my life would be difficult to maintain properly without having someone to give my love to. My scars are tangible for anyone who has ever read anything of mine. I have always made it a point to write from their point of view, because we all should begin where the pain is, healed or not. It is the only way we can satisfy this life we have. It is the only way we know what heaven could be like or what hell actually is. There is nothing more important than finding your purpose or understanding your gift. We are not an accident. Our journey is not one either. The reward for our suffering comes at a steep cost, but a cost worth paying ultimately. Love deserves to be known by all. It deserves to be appreciated by those who have gone without such beautiful things for a lifetime. I recall seeing so many faces being broken by the absence of not only love, but hope, in my time of traveling. They never have to utter a word. Between energy and lack of light, you can always tell who has it and who is still walking around, kicking the word around on the ground. Love is not only the giver of life, it is the end of it all as well. We come into this hectic scene of breathing at a rapid pace. As we begin to age, it only gets faster, then there are no more moments to reflect on. Everything seems to be reflecting back at you to show you what it is you have and what it is you have lost. Our time is momentary.

SONDER 4 5

Chapter III

-REMINISCING-

We may never get another chance at a first time of anything. I hope you make it worth it. I hope you go all in whenever you can. We will always end up losing a part or parts of ourselves in every encounter we approach. It is the absolute cost of living, of growing old in a world destined to kill you before you reach a pinnacle you feel worthy of climbing. We are the connection to every story ever told, a rambling of reflected feelings being washed away by those who take from us what we will never have again. Anything you do is precious. Anything you give your time and energy to will have a piece of you within it always. It is such a gnarly thought to have, to wake with, knowing what happens today will be the only time it ever happens. I have to take breaks from writing this book based on my own energy being used to summon these thoughts of mine. It is like when I take a vacation. It is me unplugging the power source for a week or a few days. It is a necessary tool for me to use. If I do not, I stunt my own growth as a man, as a human, as a march towards a singular victory. My mind never shuts off completely. The only time it ever did, was when I would drink or do drugs. It was a fog of life I was living in. I was never sure who would show up once I began my day drinking or filling my nose and lungs full of white lines. I created a world where it was only me and I destroyed everything and everyone else inside of it, willingly or unwillingly. I was a terrible excuse for a life. I hated myself each morning I became sober, just as I did with my mother when she would come into our rooms the very next day after one of her episodes. She would always say she was sorry, but I don't think she ever understood exactly what she had done the night before. It was my first experience with a Jekyll and Hyde personality. It was something I ultimately picked up and used in my own life later on. Over the years I have been diagnosed with bipolar, ptsd, anxiety, depression, and a few other things. It was difficult for me to hear that, but I know I had it since I was a child to some degree. You don't live my childhood and not become what you see and feel. You are subjected to chaos daily. You simply do your best to make it through and hope there is still some good parts of you left after it is all over and you're free from it. A few days ago we hit the official day of summer. Where I live, the humidity is enough to kill anything stubborn enough to believe they can remain outside longer than the sun. Take that along with the heat, it is a combination not many want to be around or live in. I've been here for seven years or at least around this area. I once thought I would live by the ocean and be a beach bum my entire life. Once you stay for a year or less than that actually, you learn to appreciate the vacations instead of the homestead it becomes. Little bits of time here and there, just enough to feed your wandering soul will be sufficient. Anything longer than that, you begin numbing yourself to everything existing in it. It is why I know my life will not have an ocean in its future whenever I am ready to move on with my journey. My father has been jobless for over 4 years now. He mentioned the other day he is pretty much retired at this point. Which is probably best for him, but it pains me to see him live here doing nothing. He works out as much as he can and then he is done for the day. The routine is a fucking killer of a man. It makes you comfortable where you thought being comfortable was a death sentence. It eats away at you one layer at a time. I know I am slowly slipping away here. I do all I can to maintain a positive outlook on life and my own desires. My mind is not the kindest of things to belong to. I used to sleep soundly without fear or worry of anything. I guess when you are a child you don't have enough living under your belt to know any different. Once you grow up, you realize just how much bad is out there for you, readying itself to infect you with its negative energy to destroy the goodness in you. I've never written a book like this before. One where it is just a continuation of thought without breaking for a long period. I have stuck to poetry and prose for the most part. But if I am being honest, I love doing this more than any other book I have done. It is a factual point of view in my life when I am taking inventory of what is really inside of my mind instead of rhyming words or making a few sentences cooperate for me. These pages will ultimately become a journal of my day to day to life, along with flashbacks to who I was before all of this and what has happened to me in a distinct and enlightened manner. I honestly don't know what will become of this book or where it will end when I am finished with it, but it feels good to know honesty lives within every word I type and nothing has been forced to sit with something it doesn't feel right being next to. If I know anything, it is love and feelings will find you when you least expect them to. It is the inevitable structure we all find ourselves in on a daily basis. It's what makes life a beautiful and strange place to coexist with another, yet make it so thought-provoking in the same breath. someone out there right now doesn't know anything about you, but there is a chance they will meet you some day and come across a face they've seen before but never could put a name to it. My own personal struggles and story has taught me and shown me how much we really don't know about this world and ourselves if we are being honest. The in and out of lies we tell to survive. The open-minded tales we speak about when we find comfort in someone else. There is something for everyone here. We just have to go out beyond the stars to reach it and make the pieces become a wholesome act of who we are. An integration of soul and bone is who I am. I will never label myself as something more than that. I believe we all have a purpose and reason for being here. Ever since I was a kid, I felt compelled to the notion of never fully belonging to one thing, but branching out to become a part of some grander visualization of purposeful living. I was never one for comfort zones. I knew you would become someone who was digging graves at an early age to make room for all the death that accompanies such ideas. We weren't made for a nine to five, a predicated schedule to live by. I also know it takes money to not worry as much as some of us do. The healthcare system is a joke and all we are doing is overpaying to be alive. Maybe that is good enough for some, but not for me. I'd rather go broke on a dream than sit behind a desk or waiting to punch out for the day. Being a dreamer only costs you your life if you're willing to go after what burns inside of you. I hope you are able to chase it all and become someone you are proud of. Someone who has been through enough tragic endings to finally believe in a beginning you can make brightening and authentic. At the end of the day, being laid up in a hospital, costing yourself hundreds of thousands of dollars just to survive is not what I am after. It costs more money not to die than it does to actually live. I have never understood it. We may never get back to the place we share ourselves with another so openly, unafraid of the consequences to follow. We go in, all in, rolling in like thunder on a summer's afternoon. We hope there is time for us again. A time when the hurt we feel today becomes something beautiful to use tomorrow for a better beginning. We are all full of stories untold, of feelings we will never utter for whatever reason. We think keeping it in makes us stronger in some way. That we have the power to keep it all at bay before the storms find us again to add to the breaking. I wish we could listen to ourselves as often as we openly listen to others. Their problems become ours unknowingly later on or in that exact moment. We carry it all down the road with us. Picking up a few flowers here and there to decorate what is already turning us into a darkness we can barely stand to be a part of. I hope you are able to cut yourself off from unwanted attention, unnecessary burdens to carry along the journey. We can only take so much until the only room left within us is barely enough for the trauma we hold onto to give us an edge in life. It is impossible to forget about everything that's happened to you. I've been to therapy a few times for my ptsd and other issues. I know it helped me enough to understand the things I was carrying were never mine to carry in the first place. But even after I was done with my sessions, they stuck to me like the flesh I was already wearing. You cannot escape a life you were meant for, just as you cannot escape those who are meant for your life. We tend to believe anything someone tells us if it fits our narrative, if it makes us feel lighter in some way. If only we could believe ourselves as easy, too. Maybe destiny is nothing more than believing in things happening for a reason. Maybe it is enough for us to attempt to chase after what was never here in the first place. I'd like to believe we all have the power needed to achieve even the most insane aspirations we are greeted with on a daily basis. Love has conquered all, and in time, we will know victory for ourselves.

Timing is everything or it can be nothing more than a failed proposition between a heart and mind that never agree on anything. I've been led down roads where someone I truly loved told me hope was awaiting. I eventually learned to admire the scenery more than what I found at the ending of it all. But all things stay with me. Especially a shared sunset with someone who loves to imagine beyond the realm of finite possibilities. There is a certain madness that is needed for life. You do not need to be put inside of a white padded room to go crazy or made to believe you are crazy. Other humans do a brilliant job at it already. You will need to lose your mind a few times to know the difference between what's good for you and what's beneficial for your future. There are multiple outcomes in today's society for those who wander beyond the edges others have drawn for us to keep us where they want us, where they can control us. We are not animals in a circus. We are the weapons in the hands of every confined beast. Do not become a tragedy based on someone else's story. Be a hero or heroine. The choice is always ours to choose which side of the line to stand on and which side of the line will be the rope we use to gain back what we lost. Take solace in soldiering on. Save face with truth wrapped around a golden blade. The sword is ours to use. Another day when I find myself more thankful than the last. My mind sometimes doesn't allow me to sit still and savor what I have done. It is always a tug-of-war between my thoughts and feelings. I know I am worthy of something good sticking around, for the goodness of something to hold me longer than this day is long. My depression gets the gets the best of me and tells me I am not any good, that I am unworthy of victories, however small or big they are. I know what I am doing matters. I know what I am doing is what I was meant to do with my life. My purpose took me an entire lifetime to find and almost was too late in finding it. I do all I can with the time given to me to write in a forever state of mind, because I know maybe something withstanding will come from it. I know something has the potential to inspire someone who feels as I do, and did. I want to be there for everyone, even when I can barely be here for myself. It is such a transient transition from dream to reality. A reality laced with impossible endeavors based off of what my aspirations are. My hands seem to be moving at all times. Creating shadows or words. It doesn't matter, because I know the intention they serve even though they aren't anyone's to hold at this moment. Love seeps from me and has broken my bones before. I still cradle it gingerly, with the softest of sighs to make sure I don't knock it off of the tree it found to rest on, to nest upon, awaiting the next breeze to use to get it to where it is needed. I could go on about what it means to me, but all I have to do is say her name and all of it comes back to me like a wandering heart tends to do when restlessness tries to comfort parts of it only she can and ever will. There is such a sadness attached to a grieving soul. Be it in loss or in absence, there is and will always be a darkness following it around. I can only hope it doesn't scare away those who are meant to be here. Though who and what is meant to find you, will. There is nothing in heaven or hell that can stop those encounters from happening. It isn't called fate. It isn't called destiny. They are all precursors to the inevitable. I do not have a word or know of a word that symbolizes its meaning. The best I can come up with is, **somox**. It means to have known what you have now in your life, would have been there regardless of any other choice or choices you would have made. I believe in everything under the sun. Even if it should parish in its own flames, I would still be here, speaking of its truths. I have a difficult time with my emotions. It is why I drank as much as I did to try and harness them in whatever way I could. Obviously it wasn't my greatest decision or revelation. I only did what I knew how to do, what I was taught, what I had seen prior to becoming the age when life begins to run you down and out of your skin.

All of my regrets in the last twenty years or so have been because of the outcome I could have been more responsible with. I don't know if it would have changed anything or any other formality could have worked. I know my purpose is finally foremost in my life now. I know my words matter, even if I am the only one who reads them. At least I am making the effort to create a better life for myself when the last thing I wanted was to move on from a love I thought I would have a lifetime to write about, to speak about, to live with. I cannot express it enough to you than saying love is more than life itself. It is the breath of the wind upon your face after waking up hungover and fucked over from the night before. It is the tender way strands of hair lay upon your chest when she is looking at you and you look back at her knowing what you two have together will never be found again. Fitzgerald once wrote about never finding the same love twice. I believed it before I knew about his words. I knew it the first time I fell in love. I knew it the last time I fell in love. Nothing in this life happens twice. It may feel as though it was as good as it was before, but nothing will ever compare to the first time lips touch souls and words touch hearts. There is no replica. There is no other way to live a life fully if you are not doing it for love. I hope you do not cheat yourself when it comes to finding it. I hope you expose your entire bone structure to its power and grace. It will not only heal you, it will demolish every castle you ever built inside your ribs and on the outside of your eyes. I know nothing if it isn't a related member to love. I know nothing if it isn't her I am trying to find, over and over again.

I understand she only exits in one form, but I see her constantly. In the face of someone else. In the sun when I am blinded by its rays and contemplating how it became what it is today. I see her in the moon, and every other phase it needs to be complete. I see her in the words, in the books, on the fucking walls. These shadows are a motherfucker I'll tell you. They want to eat at you until there is nothing left of you except the idea of who you were before this moment. Knowing what I know now, I would have still chosen her. I still would have risked my life all those times to have a single chance with her. We make our own beds before we even have anything else to sleep on. We know the decisions we make will either lead us into hell or somewhere that the devil has died trying to get into. I wake up and hope this day is the one where it all works out.

I cannot tell you how many times I have given my breath up in order to achieve a dream. I remember being a young boy and thinking to myself if it ever gets better. If there is something we as humans can do that turns all of our nightmares into a story about making it to a place when nothing hurts anymore. I have yet to find it, but I came close when I traveled to Utah for the first time. I had heard stories of that state. How it is Mormon country and the religious overtones of it all would be a turnoff. I never knew of its gargantuan beauty and its limitless power over the soul. Before I crossed the state-line, I knew this place would be somewhere I could see myself living one day. I knew it would be home to me eventually. Over the course of the two weeks I was there, it turned out to be the only thing I could think about until I got back there later that year.

When it comes to beauty, magic, love, pain, misery, it all derives from a certain core development or lack there of when we arrive at a place in our lives when balance is non-existent. It all stems from a lack of courage or communication as to why we need what we need and how we can attain said things without it becoming a chore or weigh heavy on the heart. I don't wish anyone to know my life as well as I've personally and intimately lived it. Moderation is nothing more than self-preserving your love until you're ready for it, until you know it's all you need. I haven't always done the right thing. I have barely known any good thing to ever exist without it being destroyed a few times. I do my best with what is given and what has been taken away from my life. I hold onto everything with all the fucking strength I have, because it all matters to me. It is all valuable and cherished. I've been that way my entire life. As I have gotten older, I realized how you need to and must let go of things no longer serving you or giving you peace. The ghosts we carry along with the skeletons we cannot bury, all need to go and be removed from your life if you are to ever formulate a new one to speak about. If you ever want to live again, you have to release the death you keep between your fingers, squeezing out whatever life is left within it. We cannot undo what we have done. We cannot run from the past as if it won't catch up with us. The distance we travel in thought is far greater than the one we make with our own feet. Today is a Sunday. I have been making fried rice the last several days. I finally remembered to buy chicken yesterday, so today it will be chicken fried rice again. Out of all the comfort foods I enjoy, it is hard to beat that cuisine. The only other food I hold close to it or enjoy just as much is pizza and pasta. Italian food has a devastating hold on me, and I am okay with it. The small pleasures in life make all the difference. I hope you have a few in your life. I hope you enjoy things others don't. It is what makes us who we are. It is the defining line in the lines we wear on our face from the laughs and tears we cry. We are human, and nothing more than that. Yes, we have a soul. Yes, we have organs that fail us way before it is our time to go. Yes, we are bodies composed of cosmic variables. For Christ's sake, we have universes in our eyes. How can one not be romantic when it comes to living when everything we have been through has led us to this exact second when we think about doubting it all. It takes time to appreciate the outcome, but remember, nothing is final except the last breath we take. when that comes, it will live on forever along with the words and teachings we have brought along with it. It is another sunny day here. Wind blowing the trees and what is left of the leaves from this extreme heatwave. The grass is dying all over town. The grocery stores are still pricing things as if we all have an extra million or so in the bank account. The cost of life and living these days almost makes me wonder how anyone would want to bring a new life into this world. I do not understand how any of this is sustainable when the government and governing body is against us. I haven't voted since I was eighteen and that was forced upon me in some ways. I couldn't give a shit about politics in any scope. I loathe those who base their lives around it. I guess we all have to be fanatic about something. The days are moving rapidly. More so than I can ever remember before. I am sure I said something similar to someone last year, but it is true, the older we get, the more time seems to not actually exist. Days and nights feel the same. Waking up is still a miracle we all take for granted. We go to sleep and then wake up. What a fucking dream it is to be this way. When I was a kid, I didn't worry about anything. I was fearless in every way possible. Now, I can barely go a second without thinking about death or being covered in anxiety about the simplest of things. Life is a cruel fucking mistress. It cares only about the status quo. I know it could be easier, less harmful for my own mental state by doing away with anything not choosing me. In my life, I have always felt an obligation to others before myself. I have always felt as if I wasn't giving my time and energy to something else, I was wasting it. I sit around the house on Sundays and think about the times I could have made a better choice with the choices I had previously made. There isn't a tormented way about it. It is what has happened to me because I chose it. I didn't necessarily choose the ending of how it all played out, but I sit with it long enough to appreciate the way it happened. The connectivity of it, the symbolism it now plays in my life. Every variable and variation of what could have been. There is no time for remembrance most days for those who live quickly, beating down the sky for more stars to look past. I am a moon looker, a star watcher, a lyrics singing at the top of the lungs on every roadie I take alone. Therapy comes in a lot of different forms, in a lot of different sets of eyes.

Sometimes, all we need is for someone to acknowledge us and we are made whole again. Other times it takes a few years of discovering a new breathing technique to go along with a new movement of forward. We are constantly being bombarded with information, new ideas, commercials, news, current events, anything to make us forget about who we are and why we are in the first place. We lose focus before we ever lose ourselves. It is the first step we blindly take when we encourage ourselves with the belief everything will be okay in time. It is never the case. Time simply exists to remind us of what and who is no longer here. It becomes nothing more than a reference point for us. Nothing more than a timestamp, a hyphen in-between two numbers that define us. Going through life as if everything is immediate, that there is some type of reward for all of our trials and trauma, is the fastest way to become undone. We all hope to discover why we experience everything we do at a certain age and beyond. I have been getting into a lot of documentaries as of late. More so than ever before, simply based out of wanting to know how others have dealt with certain traumatic events. The fascinating part about it is, more than you realize endure similar hardships, similar rock bottoms, and you take it all in and apply it to your life. I've never needed more motivation for my journey. I have names and reasons as to why I am who I am today. Yesterday was my younger brother's birthday. Today is the twelfth of October. I took a month off before writing again. It allows me to keep things in perspective and give more truth to what it is I am feeling. This year, my brothers and I all have turned a year older, which is the most beautiful thing. I'm still without a love to call my own, still missing someone I may never get to know again. The strangers we all become is a wild thought to think of after it all becomes nothing. We tear everything down to ready ourselves for the extraordinary, then it disappears to leave us with our bones, dreams, and all the stars to wander again. Within the wandering, we find a location that can help us and guide us. We hope we can find it before it is too late, before the hourglass gets tipped back over again for the next one who follows us. There are an infinite amount of variables that go into creating this for ourselves, as well as creating it for those who wish to join in our journey. We will never know when we are on the right path, but I can tell you how you will know, the faces you see will recognize you first.

SONDER   7 5

CHAPTER IV

-POETRY-

she's the golden hour, made from a thousand suns and a single moon. a beauty to be felt, to be seen, to be handled with a love as gentle as waves breaking over dawn. a fighter down to her bones, being broken raised her to survive a winter's cold while being okay with how alone this place makes you feel. when it comes to love, a heart must become ardent if living is what you're after. be gentle, dear child. be brave, sweet evergreen. breathing in chaos does not make you become it. it's all in the wind. it's in all of the places you feel most alive. lonely is not your name. you are infinite, as is your grace. you are cosmic, as is the love you give to every place you go and everyone who has found you here.

i could have loved you beyond the death we are all given in this life. between the darkness and light, we caught eyes and became an inseparable promise made by lovers sharing a common fight. now, all that is left of you is moonlight, every night, basking in all we once kept pressed between body and soul. you were more than an embrace during a lonely phase. you were a face making my sorrow escape this common place. i am closing my eyes with hopeful intentions of seeing you another day, in whatever life there is for those of us who hold onto the letting go coming from someone else's hands.

i remember days when i used to pray before this loneliness could find me. most of the time it was nonsense and misplaced begging that caused me to reach up to the heavens for a sign. i haven't folded my hands in over a decade, but i still hope you can hear me. when i first found you, i knew we would find our own way out. i cannot tell you or ask you   to be here, but you keep showing up and reappearing in these dreams. be it on top of me, next to me, or sneaking back into bed to warm me once again. hell is not within us or below our feet. it is right beside us. it is the place where they used to be, where love kept us, brazened and safely.

i knew i was different when my empathy became greater than my suffering. i could tell many walked around with hearts heavier than their bodies. oftentimes, strangers would find me safe enough to unload their secrets and stories from a past they were ready to bury. i could never escape a conversation brought on by honesty and rawness like an open wound. i sat there and bled with them, because bleeding openly brings humans together. it brings out a certain quality i admire in those who shed everything to feel a moment's worth of worthiness. i don't know what they see when their eyes find mine. maybe they see the child i kept alive by surviving my own hell with the help of make-believe stories and love outside of my own family. my shoulders were born to carry burdens, just as birds were made to be saviors of morning. my mourning taught me how to hold grief properly and adore those who have suffered like me. how beautiful it is to know love as a lingering thing, as a broken wing, as something afraid to breathe.

i live in these moments. the ones of you and i. the ones where distance is love, where conversation outlasts the day. i'll devour the world as it is, to give you the one you were meant to find yourself in. you may have needed to put your heart inside of a box, but i'll do all i can to make sure it lives on the outside of who you are for me. your name is grace, a sacred sensation covered in golden shine. as time draws us closer to one another, these sunrises will be our victory, as we march on like angels out of hell.

and that is how i will remember you, wide eyes with a smile changing the whole room. i looked at you while you were walking away. i wonder if you will ever think of me again. i know for me personally, i will think about a lifetime i will never get to spend with you for the rest of my time here, all the while remembering those tears running down over your smile. the ones i will never get to wipe away. the ones i will forever wear. i will move forward on the days where nothing feels as heavy as the night does when the moon comes down from its bed to visit its children to tuck us in safely and promptly. there is nothing in this world as comforting as someone who sees you and knows everything about you, and still chooses to be there with you, sitting or laying in silence for however long it takes for you to regain your breath, your calm, your direct center.

you can always start over. what you cannot do is believe someone who says you can't. i hope your courage is deep. you can die going nowhere or you can live trying to find everything you love. do not allow fear to run your life. run your life while using fear to inspire you, challenge you, mold you. do not let regret write your next chapter. close it and unearth yourself where you love yourself from the beginning to end, without pause.

in the evening when my demons are sleeping, you lay your head on this chest of mine to steady this breath of mine, keeping my soul from leaving. we never have to say a word. we both understand the value of a good thing and what love can do and become for the breaking never spoken for. be the flower potted on this windowsill of a man, and i'll bring you fresh water along with a newfangled sun to rest your enervated body on.

i try to write something down every day. i get the same urge to stay awake on road-trips because of the possibility of missing something that'll be able to help me or teach me something new. exercising the mind is crucial if you're wanting to find out who you are and what you're made of when everything else shuts down. i've been able to compartmentalize since i was a child. my storage seems to accommodate anything not helping me progress as a human. it's writing that allows me to open those doors. it allows memories and built up feelings to breathe. i wouldn't suggest this to anyone. it's how i'm wired. it's how i survive. if all i do is write down gibberish or chicken scratch for the day, i'm advancing all areas of my brain to give up what it's holding onto. if i am not creating to some degree, i feel as though i've wasted the entire day. i don't beat myself up about it if i'm taking a day off, but i still find time to jot down a few words to build off of later the next day or somewhere during the week when i feel as though it merits me to do so. my mind is made of jumbled crossword puzzles and combination locks, all vying for my time. i surprise myself daily with what i can actually get out of my soul and onto some sort of writing canvas. it's my beautiful obsession. it's how i peel back layers of earth from my eyes and truly see who i am and what exactly i'm trying to become some day. i'm a lifetime away from who i hope to be, but i'm closer today than i was years ago when all i thought i could do was fuck up everything i was involved with. it took me decades to understand how much i was unable to acknowledge my pain. my suffering felt better than any part of my emotional output. i didn't want anyone to find me, myself included. slowly i began to live again. i began to value my love for those around me. i began to take inventory of what kind of living soul was inside of me. a recreational foundation is crucial for not only your mind and body, but your spirit. we all must find things we enjoy, and maybe not necessarily love. you never want to force who you are into something you're unwilling to take the time to become. if there is a lesson in this life i can tell you, it is to never waste your birth. it is to never waste your time on those who never give you back the same effort. Small things in life will kill you quicker than anything else. do not allow someone else the opportunity to do it with you by using their heart against yours, by using their concept of what love is to them to what love is for you. never surrender your beliefs to make someone understand you.

i'll never forget what you did for me. you turned the moon into a human, into a life that will follow me throughout my life. i know some nights it will haunt me, but that's the price you pay when love becomes a woman who has to leave before you're ready for the goodbye. i held on too tight, and now, the sun doesn't even remember how to rise. now all things begin to shine during the night with eyes made of silver and gold, all howling, all defeating comfort.

i waited all night for you to crawl into my two arms. resting with our bodies attached was the only way for me to close my eyes and feel nothing for the first time all day. stay here, and find me again, sweet light. may we all arrive to the place where judgment is laid to rest beside the masks we were forced to wear when surviving asked us to be tolerable. tell me again the secret you kept in order to keep yourself alive so i can tell you the time i came back to life within your eyes. may this be all we know together. may this be what it feels like to be cared for, to be appreciated, to be told, i am here for you, i'm staying.

with water reflecting a new light,
a new and welcoming feeling, we all
must find time to respect the now,
this very paramount exuding breath.
love may find you today. it may wait
until it believes you to be ready. but
when it does arrive, never let it go.
i know how hopeless it feels to feel
nothing. i know the road is often
better felt and understood by not
risking everything for a chance to
have something more than what you
have now. be not satisfied with
normal. go out in search of love and
all its chaos, all of its unforgettable
faces. burn down like the star you are
and feel all of its glory.

i don't know what world i was made for. i don't know who will be there in the morning for me. i seem to mourn someone new every day i put on my black jeans, shirt, and cap. i think of you so fucking often, my insides beg me to go easy on feelings and just starve myself completely of the possibility of you ever leaving him for me. everyone seems to want the easy fix, the traveled path, a golden brick road, a few drinks too many to blackout and keep out of a past not worth mentioning. i'm exhausted by the excuses littered in words that die before landing in honest eyes. i don't know where to go anymore, so i'll stay inward and work on myself. i'm nothing more than a discarded Picasso, a forgotten sheet of Hemingway, doing nothing but taking up space on a good day. some won't ever understand me, but i think that's a true sign of any artist dying on a page each time to be remembered for their ability to come back to life, rather than pleasing a crowd who wants to be a part of the killing.

i've been neglecting my own life for a while now.   for some reason, i never gave up on believing you'd come back to me. but i know now i've been the author of every scar on this heart that once belonged to you. how foolish of me to care for someone who is already being loved. i never thought i deserved anyone to begin with. i guess that's what happens when you're born with a giver's soul. you go a lifetime without letting go of anything that made you feel appreciated, however briefly they stay. you learn to accept someone's least just so you can tell yourself you feel something. maybe it is a blessing in disguise for the moment it happens, but as soon as it is over, you go searching the rest of your life for scraps and crumbs to feed an appetite the forgotten taught you.

i found an old letter i wrote for you. the ones i'd write before your eyes found mine. it took me back to when love knew me better, when you held me together. it was dated and had our colors, our hearts, the nickname i gave to you. i've been told to move on, to finally place these flowers where you died in my mind, but in order to do so, you have to have somewhere to go to next, a place where you are welcomed and not shunned away for having someone's blood all over you. i wish others could find a love like we had. maybe then they'd realize you cannot say goodbye to someone who still gives you life. last night during the full moon, it was all you, just as it was from the beginning. i never thought i would get hung up on someone who beat me down like a child who stole an extra twenty dollars just so they wouldn't get jumped in the lunch line. as pathetic as it sounds. for some of us, love is all we have left to hold onto. it is the only thing worth getting up for. however horrible our experiences have been with it, the wrong one always seems to be the last to go, because of the effort you gave trying to change who they would never become.

most days it doesn't feel real. this life, these thoughts, all painful reminders of what's gone, of what may have never been here to begin with. some days it feels as if i am still on post, looking out at barren fields, wondering if i am still there, if i ever left.   war is easy. it's only when you are away from it does it become an insufferable fight. the only comfort is coming home, though a lot of us find out we never belonged there in the first place. one of the things that keeps me going is knowing this struggle is worth it, because it means i'm still   in the fight, in love with my strides. if you catch me staring off into the nothingness around me, do not interrupt or ask what i am thinking of. if you haven't seen it, if you cannot see what I am looking at, i cannot explain it to you. i am here, there, and beyond everything you believe real life to be.

i want you to care for who you are and what it took to get here. i want you to smile as if it is all you know. i want you to laugh as if you have never been hurt or been left by someone who said they wouldn't. i want you to kiss as if it is the first time, every time. i want you to view the world as you see it and not how someone swears it to be. i want you to take walks around rivers and oceans you haven't been to, but have always wanted to visit. i want you to travel to places you've never been before and take pictures of everything that makes you feel alive. i want you to cry when you need to and not hold back. i want you to drive for as long as you fucking want and get lost between here and now. i want you to fall in love with sunsets and sunrises of a new day and reflect on what has happened during your search for meaning and purpose. i want you to find happiness that makes you thankful for the heartache you have been given by those who never gave a damn about your own. i want you to feel deserving. i want you to feel complete. i want you to feel cherished. i want you to participate in your own life and not allow someone else to dictate what it means for you. i want you to tell your stories and display your art to the masses even if you only have a handful that come by and tell you what impact they had on them. you are still living and growing with the soul inside of you. i want you to be able to provide yourself with the best chance of finding out what you need in order to feel successful and close your eyes without worry. i want you to release the fears and doubts others have put in your beauty. i want you to hold onto anything resembling a source of longevity. i want you to feel safe and secure enough to go across any obstacle ever placed in front of you. i want you to be comfortable with being uncomfortable, because this universe was created in your image. you were brought into this crazy place where humans suffer for far too long before realizing how incredibly important our story is and how little we should care about opinions and beliefs of those who are petrified of challenging the rules. i want you to keep breaking them and never look back. i want each day for you to be memorable, adventurous, and tangible. that is who you will remain until the next life calls you to to teach others what you learned by being rebellious with a heart that never seemed to want to stay inside of its cage. we are the misunderstood, but understanding in our own ways. this life was carved out by our own fucking hands.

when i was a kid, i would punch walls and doors, anything that couldn't hit me back. it felt good to get that emotion, resentment, anger, and frustration out. i remember a few times i left it bloody and broken. i looked at it and thought, "why do you feel so out of place?" i haven't been able to answer that since those days. i don't punch things anymore, i write about them. it seems like it all changes except for the reason why you began in the first place. i am growing older and trying to be wiser and more mature. i am trying to understand why i was made to feel every single thing under and beyond this sky above me. there are days i feel lucky and fortunate to be me. other days i question it all. it is such a fight to stay together with yourself. i feel sympathy and empathy for anyone else who fights the way i do. as a kid, i never thought about life after the age of twenty or even thirty. as a kid, i never understood how no one else could feel the things i did or saw the things i did through eyes of which they were seen. life was made to be a struggle, and i am grateful for mine. it has taught me how not to be complacent and think everyone wants the same thing or is after something similar. i say that to say this, we are all made to feel a certain way and it isn't about figuring out why or even understanding it all. it is to live the best life we can, while we can. it is about taking those risks and chances and opportunities others pass on because they feel as if they cannot succeed. do not become your own prisoner. run your life how you want and don't take shit from anyone. you are made specifically for our own struggles. learn them and learn to love yourself through the process. i hope you take that next risk before it is another, "what if." fear is only real if you believe it to be. there is nothing that breaks a heart faster than keeping it from places it screams out to be a part of. there is no cure for the broken, except throwing yourself back into the fire to feel the flames again. there is nothing quite like the burn of knowing you are giving your all, to a cause you know is worth it, regardless of the outcome. make your tine worthy of being called a life. make your time mean something more than a single dash between two dates when the night comes and your eyes no longer open to see what you have left to do. we are the creators of a life for ourselves, and only for us. do not add pressure by attempting to build onto a home you have no room for guests to use.

not everything will make sense. that's the beauty of it. there is so much more to make sense of in the darkness and chaos because it is where some of us have been, and maybe still are. i can only hope you find your way out of it and make something memorable for the days, months, and years you have yet to live. the life we get is up to us. at times, we fail ourselves and blame others for our shortcomings. it is the destruction we all try to avoid. some of us only know how to be the mess, while others are the hands cleaning up after everyone else. there is never a right answer for the questions we seek. the only negligence existing is believing we are incapable of discovering our own truths. we are the scientists to our own illnesses, to our own adventures outside of these walls we built up around us.

maybe one day i can have
the opportunity to find you again.
some place where there is light
left in-between dusk and dawn,
in-between who we were and who
we still are. there is power in the
dreamer only a true soul can believe
in. i know these times are difficult
and feel more straining than ever
before. we must keep moving.
we must continue on these broken
roads as long as we can until
everything that has cracked before
us, gives way to new earth to love.

kissing bodies and hands wandering. licking up the dreams she had just awoken from. there is more here than he needs, but cannot stop at just kissing flesh. she lifts her hips and opens her legs to show him what he is after. the wet drip. the passion of her trembling lips. her hands wrapped tightly in sheets. his head buried deeply into a religion. he moans against her inner thighs. a vibration felt throughout the walls of her story. she lets out a mournful moan. one that finally allows the dead to sleep. one that finally sets her free. one that buries every body that has turned her against herself. peace is nothing more than intimacy when climax finds the moon being loved in the blue, instead of the gray.

something new is always exciting, but this is familiar. this is homely. that sort of thing isn't meant to be as exciting, but it is, because you are. it is, because your truth is something only angels can speak of. i know your heaviness is due to a sadness not everyone knows or has experienced. you are you, and we are this, because life made it possible to fall in love after everything before this, fell apart. my intentions were never to love you more than anyone had before me. they were set to make sure you knew how much love could hold you close, when everything else felt a million miles away. love becomes evermore when those who have it become coniferous.

i am here for the pain and beauty. for the outrageous and crazy. for the unexpected and untimely moments life gives us. maybe it is all that will ever come from this encounter. a briefness of pausing, a countering of balanced equals. a heart can only go on for so long until it, too, becomes inundated by the mundane, by the monotony of moving for the sake of forgetting. once you confess your deepest secrets, only time can allow a hole to be filled. only time can make sense of the scars and what they make us feel.

may the life you seek, always know your truth. may it always know your answer. being alive is being one with your heartbeat. within it all, fear keeps us alive. it is the precipice of adventure where we need to journey often and with intent. we find all we need when we open our eyes to things they never wish to close for. some wander because they are lost. others, because it is who they are. there is no wrong answer for forward motion. as long as we know the path will be full of trial and error, only then can we put into it what we want to get out of it.

there is only the moon left for me to give you. after all this time, her shine has lived inside of you. love is only love is we accept ourselves before anyone else. i have been able to do that since you found me underneath a sky with no stars to be seen. love is the last thing i thought anyone could give me, until you unearthed my heart and gave it back to me. we are a universal reply given to bonded souls. we are the separation of bone from flesh. we are the grave and homage paid by the sacrifices earned by our loses.

i may never be more ready to fail, to prosper, to give my all to a love i can only write about for now. i was not given this ache. i worked and killed myself almost for what it means to me to have someone like you to lay my body on the line for. i am too soft for my own good, but my bones have broken my fall a time or two after getting too close to a love not made for my blood. you are worthy of having your name spoken out loud, breaking across the sea and sky. where there is hope to be found, i will find you.

i'll never be able to write enough for you, enough about you to bring you back. i can only hope one day i'll write one that will. if you ever find yourself in need of a place to come back to, i'm here. there's nothing but hope flooding these streets of mine, so take my hand and we will swim to the other side together. until that day comes, i will keep dreaming of you wearing nothing but red. i will continue on with a mission statement stapled to the outside of my heart for every stranger to read. i know one day, a pair of eyes belonging to you will read it. be it now or fifty years down the road, i will never fall short of making my truth known and your name attached to mine. you are not a better-half for anyone. but you are what keeps both of mine free.

we both knew what we were doing. you smiled like a summer's secret, because you knew it, too. i never allowed anyone to hold me the way i let you. it was the first time i felt safety in my life. it was the first time i became more than my scars. there was a war going in side of me. a war with no end in sight. you walked right straight into the arrows, standing tall with no armor. you saw who i was and learned to love me more than the dawn adored light itself. i loved you before you said a single fucking word. some humans feel different, yet familiar all in the same breath. you made living an easy thing to do. you defeated the death hiding in me. a voice for victory, a cry for the exonerated man i became by your strength to keep me free.

maybe there was a time before this one, when we could've danced away together and forget about being born one hundred years too late in a place that mistakes fate for being nothing more than an abandoned conversation after the night ends. my hopelessness sits with a tenderness given away to a passing glance once belonging to you. under a moon with a fullness poets die to find, i laid with you, inducing the night to remain young forever. as we slipped beneath the chaos for cover. i may never be as good as i was to you. i hope betterment becomes more of a truth and less of a secret kept by the lips promised to never perish under a false pretense of love. may we be the fire instead of ashes love can leave behind for second chances.

there is magic in this world not everyone gets a lifetime to enjoy. for some of us, all we get are a few moments here and there leading us down a path of miracles and glorious memories of a world that gave us more chances than we deserved. we are the breaths that every star has ever used to believe in something real and call it human. we often forget how incredibly short this ride is. one day we are kicking and screaming, unaware of death and the pain waiting on our growth. it only stops because we choose to believe we will find a way to make peace with all the devils walking amongst us. we do everything we can to not become one ourselves. if i had an opportunity to tell you one thing, it would be to never back down from the giants we'll have to face and always look at everything as if it is an uncommon beauty. at the end of it all, it is the only thing keeping life in our eyes and love from becoming an undefeated enemy.

my confidence isn't what it used to be. i've grown weary from all the doubt inside of me. second guesses can ruin every good thing finding its way to you. some of us never feel worthy enough for them to begin with, which is why we break it before it ever makes us feel less alone. i once hung myself on a thread of neon lightning to feel the shock of being alive. it was during a time when i fought every day to stay relevant while walking the line. to this day, i'm constantly reminding myself how to approach light without flinching. my honesty isn't a welcoming most hold room for. everyone seems to be in-between weddings and funerals. you hope to catch them after the flowers have been caught and fresh earth has been spread over the top of memories. not many know what to do with an exposed human. not everyone enjoys seeing the guts it takes to survive today.

there are ways to find the love and purpose we are alive for. an open heart becomes a lifeline for those born without an ability to be more than a face waiting in line. take the hand of the moon and begin to breathe in the life you were meant for. may love always feel like a brand new day with a thousand suns burning just for you. may the love you were born with, continue birthing a cosmos for your soul to run to, play with, and learn from.

tell the angels there are ways to dance around the flames without becoming them. the crown you wear reflects a beauty, an immense fondness for triumph. maybe all there is in this world are endless possibilities beyond the wildfire in your eyes, directing a sunrise, beating down the night. i hope your courage remains alive and infinite when despair tears a hole in your heart, as love slips away with everything you had been keeping for the right time.

as the light breaks wide open, you should know my hope is to be yours by morning. my dream bleeds in color, hoping to find your body somewhere close to whatever it is my bones feel most at home. i believe in truth, and yours is my favorite to hear. i believe in all things, and when they approach me with your beauty, i remember you fondly, during a time when we both had something more than we do now. infinite love is neither lost or gained. it is something we discover when we pause long enough to allow it to find us in the waiting. seasons of change creates a stronger human, a more defined approach of living with embers to keep you warm and alive. sometimes, it is a single fading flame keeping you upright and against a starlit sky.

every night i go to bed still full of words to say and nowhere for them to go. i want to believe they dissipate into the dreams, into some foreign space outside of this world. i want to believe there is a reason for this fullness beyond the writing, beyond sitting with feelings you cannot disclose to the one you love. i awake each morning, thankful for this gift of seeing and feeling everything. it's what keeps me balanced. it's the reason why my heart will always be heavier than whatever else i am carrying. i don't believe i've ever lost love. it's stored away. it's kept from me until i learn how to express it correctly. i may have lost you in this lifetime, but i've gained an extra one to carry, to keep things safe for the both of us.

i wish you had been able to stay. i miss the way light would find your face as we both awoke to another day with each other. you'll always be the sweetest feeling for the soul in me. you'll always make waking up mean something more than the breath i take in to know i am still alive, still wondering what else is left in store for us to become. i remember the million little things you did that made me love you even more. today, they haunt me, just as the absence of you wraps me up in fear of losing more of what we were, more of what it was you made me believe was real. i wish i had not listened to you when you told me forever was all there was. i now know forever is nothing but a single breath taken when a memory holds your lungs captive.

may you never forget the beauty you're made of. may your wings never touch a patch of darkness along your way. the wild you chase after, is the kind that created you. live fully, in a wholly composition of light and truth. trust in the journey and you'll never be without the rising sun to guide you home. may its colors blind your doubts and fears. may it forever burn off what doesn't need to be in your world. i can only hope for more luminous days ahead of you and wherever the path takes you.

turn back into me. wrap your entirety around the entirety of me. i'll be here, waiting, giving all i can to the parts of you that need what you are craving, what you have been without your entire life. promises are not mine to make. all i can do is be here in present form, walking with you until you lead me further or lead me away. either way, i am as much of you as you are of the moon we sit under, making sure her love is a part of both our lives. if you decide to leave me one day, it will be how   i remember you, crescent, full, or gone completely.

i wish i was better at being yours. i wish your fears never appeared and your screams would quiet long enough so you could sit with the silence you are searching for. i love who you are, but sometimes, love isn't enough for the living left to live. what we are going through, no one else will ever know. maybe that is the most difficult part about it all. it is what makes our story worthy of being told when we are ready to tell it. until then, i will wait to add the ending of what we are doing. i will wait with a hundred handpicked flowers to give to you and vows a mile long to say to you when salvation comes.

i know your heart has been through it. i can tell by the words you choose to use to describe it. lay your body down next to mine. allow time to love us back together. there is nothing we cannot achieve together, but i am fucking exhausted being the only one who believes it. you made up your mind, as well as mine, before i had a chance to fight for what was no longer here, for what i had already loved all of my life. since you let me go and left me with nothing but empty space, all i have now are the stars. i am hoping they will be enough when the next full moon finds me and shines on these dark times i am consumed with. i hate that i allowed someone to love me this much only for them to exit when they needed something else. in all of my years of war, you have been what almost killed me by far.

i'll keep coming back to you. stay free. stay in the opening. remain in the openness. never close in the love you want to be closest to. you're too much for this world, but never enough for me. the feeling you feel of being too heavy on the inside with a soul cast out to an unknown part of a suffering, is the same one i was born with. it is why i walk on my hands when i need to feel something other than my feet going nowhere.

this world continues eating itself. i haven't had a proper meal in months. investing in solitude as the only currency i am currently carrying, i need distance from my soul and heart. i need to know there is still love between them, when the last few years have felt like an unwarranted divorce of everything i have ever belonged to. i do not want to be away from who i am longer than i need to. it becomes scary once you look in the mirror and see nothing staring back at you. i had not idea where i would be without you. i just hoped it would be me standing above the loss with hope in hand, awaiting whatever would find me next.

i wanted there to be love between us. not what i feel now. not this. the pace of my days have slowed, which is necessary for new growth, new plans to hatch themselves. there's been a lot of congestion here. i need time alone, away from everyone to practice living again. to ensure myself of properly existing before i end up coughing up the home i was buried in all of those years ago.

live for the now, for the curtains opening to reveal to you the act that will save your life. we aren't all where we want or need to be, but patience gives us the flowers to give to ourselves once we make it. bouquets of enchanted wander, of infinite gathering of magic and hope. we are given a name to go along with a body before we understand what either can do once we put in the work and sacrifice. maybe in another life none of us will know how it feels to be left behind for a reason never given. they may believe it is called protection, but all it is, is a shot to the back of the head.

prepare yourself for love. build your walls if you must, but leave an opening in the middle of it. give it a chance to run wild, to fly freely, should the right soul appear in a reflected promise and truth. do not build up to the sky. do not hide behind it for the rest of your life. you will miss out on the stars, on the moon, on anything trying to check on you to make sure you are okay and growing into an older version of time.

there's no such thing as too much of anything. moderation is for those unable to sustain progression. i learned the hard way what happens when you resist telling someone how you feel. when you feel it, do not sit with your heart unexposed. vulnerability is life, and life is the art imitated by it. i am the happiest when it is just me and my baby blue typewriter. it is the only time during the day when peace is not forced and a calm is nothing more than bleeding myself dry of every emotion hiding within who i am today. give yourself every chance to succeed in this life. we owe it to ourselves, especially those who had been told they weren't good enough for it.

never believe the thoughts that tell you, you do not deserve now. do not stumble, crumble, and fall away should you become stuck by intentions you do not understand. be thankful for the questions they bring. be thankful for the truth that comes from failure. we are nothing more than a product of fate continuing to progress as far as our minds can lead us. i wish for you to know how to hold everything you love dearly and without fear of losing it, because the truth is, everything lost will be returned at some point in a different way that you will keep closer.

kiss me and tell me what you
need. kiss me and show me how
it feels to become overwhelmed
with inexhaustible sensations.
stay here with me. your hand is in
mine, always. never too tightly.
never in a crushing stance. intentions
become more than words once you
make the effort to change or become
a grander version of who you are
together. with your head between my
shoulder and jaw, i felt nothing but a
breath i would die to protect.

maybe there will be more days for the
sun to shine and the moon to come
back to me. i may be hopeless in all
aspects of life, but everything is
gracious when it comes to feeling
something for life itself. i will never
know what it is like to love you in full,
but i once loved you from a distance
and it nearly destroyed me in every
dictation of the word. love can be
anything you want it to be. i didn't
need more time to know what i
wanted it to be with you.

since you left, i've been stuck with these memories. i can neither speak about or write about them in naked truth. i'm drowning in all this absence, in all the ways one can when love exits the room with who you were and brings out someone else you are unfamiliar with. may we see behind the mirror, behind the walls, behind anything obstructing our view. you are someone i will talk about forever, in good, and in passing once i finally move on from you. if i could tell you anything one last time, it wouldn't be, i love you. that is fucking obvious at this point. i would tell you, may you always know the moon's light is in your favor.

if you listen closely, you'll hear all of the stars open up and speak your name. wholly and holy. i've been down a million roads, but never came across anyone like you. feverishly, i search in every city you've been to get to know you better, to see who you were before the moon found you. don't find me just yet though. leave me here in this soil, undisturbed and forgotten. i have more growing to do, more growth until i am ready to walk again on my own, next to you, in all the ways souls glide across the earth.

you showed me how love can be more than a closeness. you taught me how it can be a pair of arms and eyes that hold you beyond the miles between us. you taught me how a sensation can be made to feel by simply moving your eyes to see me better. i fell in love with you long before a gesture was giving. you had me in every way, then left me all the same.

i know it hasn't been easy being the strong one all of the time. you may think you weren't made for it, but those who were lost before you, thank you today, and love you through it all. they are better because of you. i am better because of you, regardless of how much my heart has gone through since losing you. pain is an extension of love, and my limbs are all over the pace trying to find new ground to hold.

hold onto me, onto everything you believe me to be. fly with me to the moon and beyond the space between the stars we've already found. i'll love you there, continuously, indefinitely. hold me as close as you can when it comes to letting another human listen to what makes you afraid, to what actually hurts inside of you. there is plenty of room at this table i try and eat my meals at. i may not have a lot to eat, but i do have conversations should you wish to wait with me to dine. i will close my eyes, count to ten, and maybe then there will be someone who will play along with me. someone who can take sarcasm and dark humor to be a love language. i will see how long i can hold my breath after eleven comes and no one shows.

look to me when you feel as if you cannot go on anymore. i'll show you how scars are our light, how they can save us from the pain they once caused us. they are proof we have dared to love. they are proof as to how capable we are to living and enjoying a life fought for. they are the markers we all show and tell when someone asks you who you are and where you are from.

we are the breath and body for someone else. trust your heart to carry it and care for the love that finds us all at some point in time. you were mine. bad timing or wrong phases, days were longer when i knew you better and could hold you. you took away a nightmare and brought the ability to rest with your life next to mine. a softening sense of comfort, you were, and you will remain.

we gathered each other in our lives and began making plans to spend forever and a day making sure we were never without the other. simpler times they were. undying love, it was. never-ending became a story we told each other to ensure our hearts were in it for the long haul. i know how often my darkness swallowed the stars, but it all stopped the night i met you. a defender of light, you are. a defiant to all things devilish and demon-like, you are. saving grace was never a face until it found yours to trace.

i don't know where you came from or
how our souls knew to find us in this
life, but connections like this only
exist after death. we have been
born again, two humans crawling out
of the darkness we were once
consumed by. teach me how to hold
flowers without killing their essence
and i will   show you how to plant a
garden where they rise   with a moon.
friendship will always be   more
and mean more between us. we are
the life and   love of anyone who has
found a human to call home. always,
in all ways, for fucking ever.

i know there's a chance of never seeing you again. it's what creates this urgency inside of me to write all i can for you until there's not a reason to anymore. you are going to haunt me, entirely. you are going to go under with me to the abyss where life becomes a story told to waves passing through and over the boats we once belonged to. my brokenness was a beautiful war worth fighting for. i will never be ashamed of what it took to get here, what it took to be yours even if it was briefly.

take these hands and give them purpose, give them timing when all else falls between them like a second hand being removed from every breath taken. there will never be another like you. that is why goodbye isn't today. it is something lived forever in a day, and the days upon the years weighing down this smile glued and pasted on my face. happiness was never my thing to begin with. but when it came to you, there was no other way to feel, no other thing to believe in than knowing the beauty i was pressed safely against, was keeping my heart inside my chest.

made by the broken, but still in love with what remains. when one thing is taken away, we must master another. we must go where no one else can lead us. there we will find the bones of who we are and the soul of the departed, forgotten, and lost. if we can make it one more day, it will become the greatest one we've ever had. some people come into your life to give you excuses. others become the reason why you will stop listening to your own.

i've been keeping in the wind and all of your movements. as the moon loves, i love. as the birds rise, my life no longer feels lifeless. i've regained all of my misplaced belongings, because of your uncounted steps towards me. many will never comprehend my silent screams, the nightmares lying awake, awaiting someone that never comes. you'll never know pain until you're in your own grave, dying to stay warm. your grace has kept away everything, even the last handful of dirt being thrown in by my ghost.

not all light is created equally. you've always been a keeper of things, a sensitive soul yearning for more love, more space, and every star. life is not usually kind to those with a heart larger than their body. you've tried your entire life to make sense out of the loss, the empty space you feel. where one feels nothing, another feels wildflowers, a beautiful constructed constellation of hopeful power set to become the crown worn by the chosen. you are not the grief you carry. you are the mighty wings which fly above it all. be the bravery, kind soul. be royal gold.

you've bared your scars for long enough. your fight is done, my love. you've won every battle, every war. even if you feel depleted, there's more victory in you than conquering kings. you've always been the keeper of valorous light, of a mindset given to the gods. my curiosity was struck in the face by your beauty. on the twenty-fifth, you were given breath. that same breath fills my cup now, overruneth. it all becomes endless once we begin to find parts of ourselves others had been thieving during nights of lonely.

pull me under, beneath who you believe yourself to be. take me to your roots, to your last defeat, to the last someone who was never going to love you the way you needed to be loved. pull me under and through. all the way to where you and i become something the devil and death laugh about. knowing what we are, cannot die or be undone. i'll show you how poetry can be a human, how it can outlast all the stars. i'll never not be reaching for you.

most days i am okay with feeling this way. i am able to manage the pain that comes along with everything else i have saved from a disturbing upbringing. it seems as if i am in a staring contest with depression. a game i lose constantly, then have anxiety tapping my shoulder saying, me next. a body like this never rests properly. a mind like this should've caved in a long time ago, but a chance to be yours some day, well, it's the only beautiful thought still fighting, still giving me a lively pulse to call living. as long as the moon is on my side, i'll never be without love, without light.

this fever will never break for you. consumed by nothing more than an accidental encounter, we pursued each other. today, we are ghosts in sheets, pretending to scare away the demons we were forced to keep. you told me you saw me as a keeper of rare things. i laughed and told you the same. i'll try and hold onto you for as long as i can. when rarity finds you, sleep comes easier, life gets clearer, and a fairy-tale is born in your heart. she'll always be the glass slipper in my story, and everything righteous before midnight strikes.

i knew it was going to be you. even if you ended up walking away one day, it was you my entire life. humans speak of soulmates and twin flames as if that's all that exists in this world. when you meet the one, the familiar sight of knowing you found morning again, knowing life didn't abide by your request of dying just yet. you were many things to me, but you are still the reason why i'm alive. why every day matters more than before when i look for you between sunset and sunrise, finding new ways to tell you, i love you, without breaking the sky in-half.

may love always be in season. may it always keep its feelings within reason, within a steady motion of truth and believing. there is strength in solitude, but we all need a certain warmth from a body whose fire is not made to burn us. you are not your thoughts. it's something i've been told since i was young. we still need to be reminded of it, even after our hearts are done bleeding from the open wounds. be brave, always. we are born to carry more than our shoulders tell and show us. but i must tell you now, do not become the weight or the burdens you haul through life. instead, become the wings of a love song, become a hallelujah spoken right before the eyes close and hands open wide.

SONDER   1 5 1

Chapter V

-REFLECTIONS-

I wish I could tell you a million things and you would believe them. I have wandered this earth several times over and I cannot come to any other conclusion than this: We are created. We attempt life. Love is guaranteed to break you for worse, for better. There is nothing about being here that makes anything we go through easier. We are all suffering in our own little quiet worlds. Blinds closed most of the time to keep the onlookers outside from catching glimpses of what we don't want others to see, afraid if they ever did, they'd know more of our weaknesses than the ones we already show. We are a silent bunch, mad to the touch, but lazily confined to our ideals and beliefs. We are taught at an early age how this life we live came to be. how this world grew from roots planted deep into space. How gravity exists, but only while we are here.

I'm not sure if those who told me things like that, ever experienced a life like mine. I wonder what qualifies them to tell me what I already know, as they attempt to destroy my mind and corrupt my soul like a cheap bottle of wine on a nightly stroll downtown. We hope we have time to correct what we have gotten wrong to some capacity. We hope we are given another day to make headway in this journey. There is light and dark. There are devils and those who believe in angels saving us all from open flames. My feet hurt. My back hurts. My mind spirals daily around such things. I don't know if I was born to be twisted up and knotted into a million different reasons for others to pull at me. I am not as old as those who waited a lifetime to pursue their destiny, but I can feel my body sway with every rotation this earth makes. I've tried my entire life to reel in my own feelings and feelings of those around me without them becoming my own. I live a thousand different lives, daily. Each one asks something different from me. Each one is laced with a victory somewhere near the end of the sun's duty. I live my life in pain, in a daze of what I want to say and what I keep to myself to allow a smoother transition, step by step. I was a wild child, never afraid of any consequences due to my rebellious ways. My habits created who you see today. I've been able to keep a hold of several that almost got too far away from me. I've lost so many to the fact that I was unable to control myself, my actions, my words, my involuntary acts of becoming more dangerous than the day prior. I know there is still more for me to do out there, more roads to travel and finding places to write about.

I look forward to those days most, so in a lot of ways, I'm wasting my own life, wishing for tomorrow to arrive quicker before my past catches up to me. My anxiety has become uncontrollable at times over the last several years. I know I need help in that area, but I know what the pills do to me and my mind. A cloud hangs over me and follows me as I try and type out more of my soul so it can breathe and have a better life than the one I am currently living. Today is the second day of July. In a few months it will have been three years since I moved back to Texas. I never imagined myself being here this long. I never knew I would be stuck here again to fend off all of my demons in the same house I once felt trapped in, day in and day out. I don't want to leave my dad until I find a way out of here for him. I also know my needs have to be met, and there is nothing left here for me besides my dad. I wake up, go to the track, walk at least ten circles around a blue semicircle, come back, work out some more, then begin my day. This routine is blasphemy to the life I am trying to make for myself. I am saving money, yes, but we are not meant to be paralyzed by the life we currently have. There is supposed to be freedom within us and beside us to help us further our own breath. The sun shines brighter most days. The ocean is less than ten miles away from me. I haven't been in a few years. I am tired of the sea life. I am at my wits' end with the monotony that has found its way to me. I do all I can to remain sane, to remain active in every aspect of my life, because I know the alternative is worse than the worst day I've ever had. I remind myself to breathe and carry on. Once we are in the fight, once we are born, we adventure into a livelihood of staying alive by any means necessary. Going to war changed my entire perspective as a whole. The first day we were in country, I heard the initial gunshot. No one knew who got shot or if someone got shot. No one knew if it was the enemy who fired it or if it was friendly fire. I later found out what had happened, but as I stared down the sights of my M249 SAW, in the prone position, on the side of a dirt mound, I knew life was happening in the realest of terms. I knew war was a real and tangible thing. I was twenty-two and a boot in the Corps. I quickly learned how war was and what it was, while laying there, trying to take in every sound around me and every moving thing that might have been the Taliban. We moved positions soon after. Another ten to fifteen miles with close to or over one hundred pounds of gear on. The air tasted different. The sweat evaporated before it thought about falling from your skin. It was silent most of the day, but hell tends to be that way when all of its soldiers are out making life an impossible thing. Most devils are born silent, then learn to kill. There is never an easy way to become who you need. There is only the act of becoming and whatever it brings. I wish someone had told me how difficult life would be once you got out of the military. Unfortunately, I was discharged after three years. The month I was handed my punishment, November of 2009, the following week we got orders informing us we would be going back to Afghanistan once again. I was devastated. The most fucking broken I had ever been before in my life. I was truly fucking heartbroken with my soul ripped from my body. I knew

I wouldn't be joining my brothers in the fight. The same brothers I had fought with and bled beside the year prior. The ones I taught and trained with to make sure they didn't die and had all the knowledge they needed in order to make it back alive. I not only failed myself, I failed those who I would be leaving behind once they got on the bus. I waited back on base until I was separated from the Marines. The fucking guilt was heavy. It was the heaviest thing I had ever felt in my life. The goodbyes were excruciating. I looked at them all and told them again how sorry I was for fucking up and fucking over so many by my destructive and selfish behavior. I was not sure how I was going to be able to make it. I told my best friends how sorry I was for getting them in trouble and the pain I had caused them the night I got picked up and thrown into holding on base.

These were the guys I went to boot camp with, most of them anyway. The guys I trained for on multiple OPS in the states to get ready for another war against the Taliban. I wasn't sure where this book was going when I first started it last year. I didn't want to make an autobiography about my life. I wanted it to be things I had learned over the course of my life and thoughts I've had over my life. But in order for those thoughts to mean something and be as true as I can make them, you need to know some things about my life that only a handful of people truly know about me. Before they got onto the bus, my SSGT came over to me and I shook his hand and thanked him for being there for me and training me the past year. He looked at me. Not in disgust, but pity almost. It broke me even more, because I was tagged as a

TL(Team Leader) when we got back in 2008. I had responsibility and I couldn't even be responsible for my own actions. My decision making was lost a few months after being back in the states around January of 2009. As I was shaking his hand, he looked at me and said, "Don't waste this life you've been given. Don't let yourself down by not making something of this opportunity. Do something with your life. Make these guys proud of who you will become." We talked a little while longer, but those few sentences stuck with me and still stick with me today. It reminded me of a part in Saving Private Ryan, when Tom Hanks' character told Matt Damon's character at the end, "Earn This." I replay that encounter in my head at least once a day to remind myself to be better and do better than before. To become something I would be proud of. Not to make up for my past actions, but to create a life I would be lucky to have if I had not ended up the way I did all those years ago now. I think of my brothers every day. It is my balance, along with a few other things, but they keep me balanced. Especially those who lost their lives over there that year. I always try and live my best life, because I know they would give fucking anything to be alive again. To be living and doing all thew things they'll never get a chance to do again. Every year is a reminder as their KIA anniversaries approach. I've lost so many, as has those who fought with them and their families who can only love a picture or a memory now, instead of a warm body that has the look of love in their eyes staring back. Survivor's guilt is something you never truly grasp until it picks you up and slams you down daily. I went to therapy once I got out because of it.

My drinking never got better. I'm sure I was drinking even more to drown everything else out. Mourning, missing, wishing, and anything else the day brought me, I was desperately looking not to avoid it. I was attempting to make sense of it, to understand it without it becoming a part of my entirety. Grief tends to be that way. It becomes a part of you. It becomes everything you do with your life. It is the catalyst for every action you consist of. I didn't want or need any more of it in my life at that point. I had lost too many and more than most by that age. I was already drowning. I didn't know how to escape it without escaping life, the reality I was in. Working out and keeping a busy mind helped with some of it. What I couldn't control, eventually lashed out at family members and friends. It caused my spiraling and distancing I was making with anyone I loved. Today, it is better, I am better. even on days when I don't feel okay, I know it will be, because there is nothing wrong with feeling that way. Being honest about what we feel and what is inside of us helps everyone. It takes trusting yourself, which was insanely foreign to me. It was not until 2015 when I did fully trust who I was and who I wanted to be. I became sober in October of that year. I began giving myself to my writing which found its way back to me after years of not embracing it. I had been writing on and off since I was five. It became my life, my passion, my purpose. It is what I was born to do. I may not be the best at it, but you don't have to be when you love what you do. You only have to enjoy its company and believe in it. It's the best "job" I've ever had. Life is brightly again. When fighting is all you know, you learn to adapt to any situation asking violence from you. These days, it is as if that's all we as humans are comfortable with, all we can stomach, because the last twenty-five years have taught us to become numb to it. Today is July 4th. There was another mass shooting in Illinois. Six people have died so far and another twenty-four have been wounded. I've only seen a few people post about it. Be it as what today represents, it's getting difficult to celebrate anything without apprehension. Life is precious, yet we remain in an open war daily. I wish there was more peace these days. I wish humans could get along with one another. Power is one thing. Continuing to chase after it by any means necessary to prove a point or agenda is another. My birthday is coming up in a few months. I think about my youth a lot more as I am getting older.

I remember growing up on post oak road. It was my grandparent's home, then my mother and father eventually moved into it at one point I remember jumping barbwire fences and exploring for hours without any trouble to speak of. We were all young once. Some of us live our lives to keep the child we once were alive. Others outgrow it by the time they are teenagers. Simpler times always stood out to me and gave me comfort. Chaos was absent while growing up where I was until the divorce happened. Of course there were bad times for everyone back then. Maybe I was naive to it since I was so young or I didn't give a fuck because I knew I was safe in whatever small-minded opinion it was for me to believe. Each day I get on here to write something from my heart, my soul, from parts of me I haven't opened up in years. I want to give hope to anyone seeking closure, safety, a few minutes or hours from your day to get lost in my thoughts and take a break from being inside of your own. I will be done with this book in a few months. I began this journey without a direction. I simply wanted to keep a journal in some ways to allow others to read and interpret how they want. I'm writing a few pages a day. Some times more than that. It all depends on my mood and how the energy is for me. It's been that way my entire life. Being an empath, you learn how to compartmentalize things accordingly. It took me over thirty years to realize I had that kind of power. I don't want to call it a gift, because there are days I absolutely loathe feeling everything from anyone crossing my path. Every now and then, I am consumed by the earth's energy as a whole. I feel its sadness, its tears, and when the brighter days show up, I feel its warmth and sun. I live my life with thoughts of death a lot more these days. I don't want to sound morbid when saying it, but it's how I have been for the last several years. It will come for us all and on that day, we will all be the same. There will be nothing anyone can do or change. A level playing field doesn't exist. We are either born into money or for some of us, we learn how to maximize and monopolize our gifts. The other ones who have struck out in life, the ones I see every trip I take to Southlake on street corners and underneath bridges. They are the ones who my heart bleeds for. All they know is darkness. All they have are cardboard signs with a brief message to express themselves, hoping someone stops and reads it long enough to hand them few dollars if they have it, if they make eye contact instead of pretending they aren't even there to begin with. I think about them more so during the summer parts of being here. It easily exceeds one hundred degrees for at least three to four months out of the year here in this part of the state. I hope one day money won't divide us and humanity alone can somehow bring us together. I've traveled enough to know how lonely this world can make you. How incredibly cruel it is to those who wish to dream outside of their minds. A starving artist is who I am, even though I live with my dad. It is my way of life. Sometimes I get a few orders in a day. Other times, I can go a week or so without making any money. I never put value into it. It stems from my childhood when we didn't have enough to be comfortable. I'd go over to my best friend's house and there was a pool, a few ATVs, and all the food you could eat.

Growing up where I did, you either had old money or your land sat on oil money. The only in-between was moving there while having money. My dad worked away from home all of my life. My mother did all she could to get by on what he made, while making sure we had new clothes and supplies every school year. I've worn the hand-me-downs. I've went to school with my stomach growling. I've never had to beg for a thing in my life except love. It's been the one thing I could never get enough of, regardless of how many times it left me broken and bruised beyond recognition. This life is nothing more than learning how to unfold with the chaos. It is about learning as much as you can about yourself in every situation you're placed in and involved with. I've worked all over the states. Construction, landscaping, any form of manual labor was my forte. My body was broken before I got into my twenties. I manage pain better than most. My high-tolerance for it has allowed me to overachieve in a lot of ways, along with enjoying tattoo sessions as therapy. My childhood fucked me up without question, but it also taught me all the lessons I needed to live in a world as fucked up as the one we all currently find ourselves in. I wouldn't change a thing about who I am or where I've come from. All were necessary evils I shook hands with to get to the next floor in the building of misery. I know brighter days will find us if we continue trying and giving all we have to the day. The sun teaches us how to rise. The moon teaches us how to shine in darkness. The stars teach us how even though you are dying, you are still made from a light that never goes out. We are all energy. We are all angels and devils with names, with faces constructed by the pain we best associate ourselves with. Growing up, we lived with my mom's parents for a large portion of it. My grandfather, R.L., taught me more than I'll ever know from someone else. He made it the best with any situation that found him. My first memory of him was going with him to cook hamburgers and make snow-cones. He was one of the greatest men I ever knew. He suffered a lot and I learned how to do the same by watching him live his life. Back in his day, life was much more dog eat dog. If you didn't stand up for yourself, you were going to get beat down with the rest of those who fell short of being a man. I'm not the best example of that. I've fucked over a lot more people than I ever thought I would. It wasn't because I was malicious. I simply didn't know how to not be that. I was never taught or shown how to console those parts of me until I was older. And even then, I ruined those who tried to love me. Some of us are meant for ever-after. The rest of us do our best to get by with what we have and lose along the way up and down these broken highways. I'm still trying to put together a life for myself. It doesn't get any easier as you age with time. I tend to procrastinate more now than ever before. But in my head, I always feel as though I have the time down to a science. I do not put more pressure on myself to make a deadline these days. I go with the natural state of the flow and energy I feel. It doesn't work out in my favor all the time, but more times than not, it arrives right on schedule without added worries to go along with it. This phase in my life, I have put love on the back-burner. I know it will be there eventually, and I will be okay with it finding me then. Several years ago, I thought I was done looking for it. I thought my life was going to be one way, since the woman I was talking to felt the same thing. I know things aren't perfect, just as humans never will be. When you spend a large portion of your life believing one thing, then it gets cut up and thrown out of the window while you're driving along smoothly, it fucks you up like no drug ever could. I've been twisted up on cocaine and meth. On the drink and pills. All of it never left me as devastated as love has. I blame myself for putting it on such a high pedestal. It was a place I thought it belonged after watching my parent's marriage fall apart all of those years ago now. I never wanted to end up like that with someone I loved. I did everything I could not to. Unfortunately, brokenness is the way for most of us. Those who feel everything, who speak gently into the night allowing it to invade your heart and mind with fairy-tales and fate. When you grow up surrounded by chaos, you think it won't have the guts to follow you throughout your life. How fucking wrong I was to think that. It's left me dumbfounded and wounded a million times. I've sat with the sun for a while and tried to learn from it how to rise through the darkest parts of where it lives. How it crawls to the mountains for forgiveness for not being better at shining when it is called upon. Nature has always been a muse to me. All encompassing and infinite. The sights. The sounds. The freshness. The earthly tones of everything you want your life and soul to be and transform into. Calmness is not available to us all. A direct neglect of self is all we are left with when we discover how deeply rooted we are in misinformation about ourselves and the world around us. When you go from wanting nothing more than love to be your center, to wanting nothing to do with it at all, you realize how much further you have to go when it comes down to your path. Immense clearing needs to be done so you don't end up tumbling down some wooded area you do not belong. Being this age now is still a surprise to me. Waking up to another day is still jarring to me. When I was a young child, I always thought I would die before turning thirty. Don't ask me why. It was just how I felt, which is why I lived my life as if old age would never touch me. Being an empath is part of it. The old soul within me tends to move more for music and art, than humans most days. My ideas and beliefs are self-taught. My entire life I've tried to stay away from a group mentality and base my feelings and thoughts on my own experiences. I know it is the best way to approach anything new or aged. Having a closed mind is basically having a casket already picked out for you with your name on the side to let others know who you are. Each day I wonder more into the abyss inside and outside of my control. I want to dive as deep as I can into things that I'm attracted to. My solitude allows me and permits me to inhabit many faces and colors to wear along with my all black attire. I used to be the one who wanted nothing but brand named clothes and shoes and caps. I wanted to be seen as someone who had style and class without actually knowing a goddamn thing about it. A long time ago, I stopped buying those clothes. I wear the same outfit multiple days in row. I don't give a fuck who sees me out like that.

No one has ever said anything, but if they ever do, I will laugh and be on my way. For someone to come near me and ask me about my clothes is the last thing I am concerned about. I am not here trying to fit in anymore. I have no desire or need to do something so asinine. My reality is not like yours. Me trying to impress someone has everything to do with what I can come up with when it comes to writings. It has absolutely nothing to do with my selection of clothing. I traded in my car at the end of last year for a new dodge ram. I knew I shouldn't have. Something inside me told me I would need it down the road. So far, it hasn't came to be. With gas prices going over four dollars and more where I live, it was one of the worst decisions of my life. Before I bought it, I had no idea the gas prices were going to increase as much as they did, nor did I foresee the world turning into the shitshow it would ultimately become towards the new year. When you begin paying over one-hundred dollars for a tank of gas it becomes even more insane and downright stealing. What a piece of work our government is and has always been. The pandemic, shortage of baby formula, mass shootings, fuel issues, everything is pointing to the end of the world it feels like. If it were to happen, I'd honestly be okay with it. It is such a toxic place to be now. It is such a far cry from when I was still a teenager. I thought paying a dollar eighty-five was expensive back in the day. Thankfully I am not traveling as much anymore. But the reason I am not is because of the fuel prices and hotel expenses. Everyone is trying to make up for what they have lost the few years in any way they can. Gouging and fucking over the consumer in their way, by all means necessary. Crippling us all until we have no money left for bread and water. The good life doesn't exist anymore, unless you have six to seven figures already in your bank account. Maybe at some point the American dream was brought to life, stolen or bought for, but after the last three years, I am pretty sure it has been buried without a marker to show others what it once was. Greed and poverty enrich these lands now. More caskets in the ground than land to give room to them. Each day, there seems to be something else that happens to make living here damn near uninhabitable. Apartment rent and mortgages are sky rocketing. You can't even buy a vehicle for less than forty to fifty thousand. At least a new one you once bought for around thirty thousand several years ago. My truck payment is almost six hundred dollars a month. I feel ashamed even typing that. By the end of the year I will be trading it in for another Chrysler 300. Fuel mileage is more necessary than most things right now. Everyone is struggling to get by, to survive, to maintain a proper life. I have friends who have newborns who are going without formula. I feel sorry for them. It is already tough enough on your own, then adding another little human into the equation is almost suicide if you are not capable of providing. There is a heaviness that's been following me the last four years. its weight alone is crushing. Sometimes I wake up already defeated from it being with me. I wake up a lot more these days exceedingly tired than before I went to bed. It is something unusual for me. Maybe it is old age or my soul is more exhausted than I initially thought. I'm listening to Spotify right now, with Dermot Kennedy's songs being played just above a whisper. I typically don't listen to anything when I write. It interrupts my flow and state of mind. I also have a hard time with anyone else in the same house as me or area. I pick up on their energy and it ruins any thought of my own. The same goes for reading. I haven't read a single book in the last year probably. I've bought several poetry books from dead poets who give me inspiration. But I always seem tow go slow with those and pick and choose how many pages I will read and when. The way I am constructed, the more energy there is around me and material I see, the less of myself I become. I have learned how to filter and funnel most of it through certain aspects of my daily routine. It isn't easy being born this way, to walk amongst others as an exposed nerve, picking up on every sound and vibration given off. I don't mind it if it comes from animals or the shine of the day. I can be asshole about it if pressed on the subject. I'm very rigid as well, with sharp edges I've sharpened from the dead I carry. I have my ways of doing life that I've earned to keep. I still care about what others think for some reason though. It is one of the last few things I have that I hate about myself. Maybe when I am seventy I'll have made peace with that part of me. It isn't crippling nor do I worry about it as much as I once did. But I do feel it happen more times than not when I am just walking around the track or in public longer than I need to be. We are still attempting to become more of who we are and less of who we were. It is a beautiful rendition of give and take, of a two step dance in the middle of a wake. I hope you know who you are meant to be. I hope you know someone who cares about you and for you infinitely. I wish there were easier days for all of us. I wish there were better ways for us to cope with what we're going through. I hate how commercially subjected we are to anything that can numb us or make us feel as though it will be a good time. Being sober for this long, you learn more about what this world wants you to be rather what you need from yourself to become human. If it isn't alcohol, it is makeup. If it isn't makeup, it is food. If it isn't food, it's some miracle drug, another fucking diet pill that will make you lose weight by not even having to workout. What a life this is for us. Slipping further and further away from our compass to land in a place where they want us to be. Being a recovering alcoholic, I live my life one day at a time. I learned that while in rehab. It is easy to say but fucking difficult to do. To not think about tomorrow at all. To not give your energy to the "what if" and "if only." We are all harboring demons that at any moment could take us down. It is why when I see what is on tv, it disgusts me. There isn't enough outrage about it, but that's life isn't it? Only being enraged when it suits you or is something you don't like personally. Anything else we can stomach for the meantime. I'm not a religious human. I stopped going to church in 2009 after the pastor at this cowboy church my dad and his fiance at the time were going to. Even as a kid, I wasn't all about Jesus and God and the bible. Growing up in Texas, especially where I lived, it is the bible belt of America. I was raised as a southern baptist. At one point I was proud to be called a Christian. I don't align with it and haven't in a very long time. I don't judge anyone who is or does go to church.

Never have. Never will. I remember being no older than ten and seeing elderly people look down on so many who weren't the so called "perfect Christian." I don't even know what the fuck that is or ever was. I hope I never do. When pastors are making more money than God himself, something is wrong with the system. This entire world is corrupt. From the president, to elected officials, to anyone with power. It is sad, though it is the course of this version of America and all of the tycoons had back in the day. Oil money, gold, diamonds, silver, whatever it was that made you rich, your voice trumped anyone else trying to speak about truth and resisting their ways. I always wanted to be the bad guy when I watched movies. I thought it was badass to watch the bank robbers and mob members get away with things because they were not only respected, they did it their way without giving a shit about what others thought. Of course not everything they did I agreed with, but that's the point of watching movies. It is an escape. It is a free timeout from what's going on in your life, in the world. I was born the middle child, so I have had to fight for everything my entire life. I saw different perspectives each day I was out with my brothers and family members. I never understood how we all could be so different but related at the end of the day. I love them more than anything. My pride I have in them and because of them is immeasurable. What they have done with their lives after all the things we had to endure as kids, is a fucking miracle we three are still alive and breathing. Their success is one of things that drives me and keeps me on this path. I remember being in rehab, a week or so after my failed suicide attempt. I called both of them and told them. Rock bottom never felt more bottomless. It took me five years after getting out of the Marines to finally find my footing, to find where I belonged. Between there and ending up living with my father when I got out, my drinking became out of control. I was drinking a thirty pack or more every weekend to wash down the college football I was watching. I thought it was my best way to cope. If I could get lost inside of the chaos it brought me, maybe I could find a way out of it. I was struggling and my dad saw it. He kept with me though and continued fighting to make sure I would be okay when we weren't fighting. It wasn't easy. Being in my mid twenties living with my dad who is thirty-two years older than I am, brought a lot of hard times and a different life to get accustomed to. It wasn't all bad though. I was able to spend time with him and make up for lost time when I was younger and he was gone due to his work. I lost my driver's license in 2009 and didn't get it back until 2015. I had never felt more inept in my entire life. Being chauffeured around again just as I was when I was teenager created even more self-loathing. I didn't have an opportunity to take my driving test until I was eighteen. To be without the one thing that gave me independence was horrendous. It made me want to drink even more than before just to keep from having to be reminded of it every day. Life is a heavy burden for a lot of us. We carry more than our struggles with us daily. More times than not, they aren't always entirely ours to begin with. We aren't allowed the opportunity to fix any of it. We simply have to learn how to carry it without it weighing us down anymore than we already are. Life tends to give its toughest battles to its strongest of warriors, so they say. Even if you succeed, you won't make it out without scars and bruises to show for your efforts. Each day I am thankful for all of what I have accumulated over the years. I remember a time in my life when I hated everything I had ever done and anyone who had tried or was trying to help me. When you are dealing with that level of depression, you tend to lash out at anyone within striking distance. I believe mine was a memory oriented ordeal. My mother would do the same when we were younger. Always apologizing after the matter was over the next morning. You don't really understand who you are until who you are is someone you want to change, not only for a betterment, but for survival. I've lived a million different lives it seems.

Each one led me down a path of destruction to some extent. Along the way, I also found redemption and love that met me half-way which directed me towards getting out of what I thought was destined to be the end of me. I wake up with a heaviness most days. I'm not sure if it is the season we are in or if it is just the way I was made. But I don't remember days like this as a youngster. I guess freedom and life not lived to that point has a lot to do with it. Nothing is there as a marker for you to gauge what you should feel like. All you really know are two feelings: happiness and anger. Those were mine at least. It took me a while to get a grip on who I was before it got worse. Unfortunately, my childhood was only suitable for the demons I had with me. They thrived and I kept them alive by feeding them more of what they needed, instead of finding ways to make myself better. I self medicated throughout my entire life. Some days I regret everything I ever did. Other days, I am grateful for my path and the choices I made in the end. I don't have a script anyone can go off of to make what hurts them feel any better. I only know what worked for me. When I was in rehab, the first day was sketchy to say the least. They put me in a room with a recovering heroin addict. There were two beds. His was on the far side and mine was against the right wall in the room. I was up most of the night. His screams and pacing once he got up due to him not being able to sit still sticks with me to this day. I thought my situation was bad. I had never put anything into my arm or smoked anything I didn't already know about. I was in there for alcohol abuse and my two DUIs in three months, along with my failed suicide attempt, which I have previously spoken about. The food there wasn't all that bad. It was chow hall food as it was on base for the most part. We weren't allowed cell phones or mail until we got called in to go to the "house." I was in that room only for the night and then they switched me to another one by myself the next day. I never thought I would end up in a rehab facility. I had watched several movies which had them in it, so I kind of had an idea about what they were like. Even then, it doesn't prepare you for what they actually are and the kind of humans you will find inside of their walls. A lot of those I was with were military men and women. Mostly addicted to pills and a few like me with alcohol issues. I met some of the most beautiful souls in there. We went to meetings every other night. We played sand volleyball and had open mic night when a couple of them had their guitars and sang. We went to class half the day, then went back to our rooms. Some of it is a blur to me. I was in my own room for a week and then got called up to go to the "house." There were around twenty to thirty of us there I believe. I was rooming with a guy who had three DUIs and was on the precipice of going to prison because of it. Rehab was a part of the plea deal he got, but I found out later on he actually ended up going to prison for a few years. He was a huge hockey fan. Pittsburgh Penguins to be exact. It just so happened they were playing for the Stanley Cup that year. He and I would watch the games every night with a few others. The Penguins were my favorite hockey team and had been since my family and I lived in Pennsylvania when I was a kid. There wasn't much else to do at night other than walk around the facility and find your friends you had made there and talk about life after getting out. We were finally permitted to get mail and make phone calls after the first week. Cigarettes were a premium. I had never smoked so many goddamn cigarettes in my life and that's considering I was deployed to Afghanistan for almost eight months. If you weren't in class or playing a sport inside there, you were smoking and drinking coffee. I remember when I first got into a classroom setting. It held around fifteen of us or so. The counselor went around asking who were and what we did to get into there. I told everyone what had happened and the looks on their faces are stained on my soul today. Horrified for the most part. A lot of them couldn't get their heads around what I had done, but I knew if I was going to make it out of there with a new life, I needed to be as honest as I had ever been before. I quickly understood who everyone was and what they did to get themselves into the facility. I made a lot of friends right off the bat. There aren't many friends you make in life like those who share addiction issues. Some of them were closed off and afraid to speak about anything, but once you are in a smaller group, they completely open up to you about anything and everything. By the third week, a friend of mine and I were given the opportunity to bring the flag in each night before heading off to the "house." He was a Marine as well and I won't mention his name, but he was hurting pretty bad right from the jump. For the moment between walking outside to bring it down and fold it, walking it back in, nothing felt off. It was if we were at some duty station just going through protocol. My counselor,

Mary, was the sweetest. She gave you all she had and asked the same out of you. I trusted her as soon as the first session was over. They don't make many like her anymore. She would pull me to the side often and ask me about my day and my mental health. A true caregiver to the extreme, and I was okay with it because I understood extremes more than most. Towards the end of our time there, we were allowed to make phone calls to those who would be picking us up. I only had one person who I wanted to pick me up. My best friend at the time I was with in the Marines. I will never forget the day I was released from there. The sky was as blue as the sea. It almost looked as if the sea and sky traded places just for me. The trees were as green as I had ever seen. It was as if leprechauns had been there, coloring it all in with shamrocks and four leaf clovers.

Once I was picked up and drove out of there, I was a fish out of water. Being there for a month completely washed and cleansed me unlike anything before. All of my senses were firing and kicking in. I don't know what birth was like, but I imagine it was something similar to what I experienced then. My buddy and I talked the whole way back to base. It took over an hour to get back, but just to be out in society again was a challenge I wasn't truly prepared for. I walked into a convenient store to get dip and a monster, walking through aisle after aisle of liquor, wine, and beer. I told myself, don't fuck this up. Don't throw away everything you had been taught and go off course. I remained that way for six months. Living on a Marine Corps base, trying to remain sober is equivalent to being a bartender who has to be sober in order to pour the drinks, make conversation, and leave it cleaner than before you got there. Maybe that is a shitty analogy, but it is what I thought about when I got back onto base. Barrack life is something you will never understand unless you have lived it. After working or after training, it is nothing more than being as belligerent as possible, drinking as much as your body can allow into its system, and not giving a fuck about the next day, because by then, your body is trained to be a warrior's body and you can pretty much do anything that requires physical activity. In other words, if you want to be sober, going to rehab for a month won't help you even if you were the one who asked to go there. The only thing that will set you free is remaining in the mindset of knowing if you fuck up again, you won't only let yourself down, you will let anyone who ever tried to help you, love you, and be there for you. I was sober for months after getting out. Once I hit the six month mark, I felt as though I was good to go. I thought I was solid and had all the tools I needed to remain that way. I was still going to meetings once a week as an out-patient treatment on base with a few of those I was in rehab with. One night, I went to the bar with my friends and had a drink. That one drink led to another one and by the time I knew what happened, I woke up after blacking out. I still thought I was okay and could handle a drink or two. Obviously it wasn't the case. I drank cheap wine and that was all I allowed myself to have after that incident. I then went back to the house where hell found me. I had previously went back there before going to rehab to clean the bathroom where the tub still had blood rings on it and the shower curtain was stained with it as well. The suicide note I had written was still there folded on my pillow along with the CD player with the disc still inside of it. I tore it up and threw it away and I broke the CD in half and put it in the garbage. I wasn't kicked out of the house, but I knew I couldn't live there anymore. I let my three best friends down, and even worse, I broke the promise I had made to myself to not get in trouble or get my buddies in trouble. We weren't supposed to have the beach house to begin with, but Marines are stubborn that way and don't care for rules. The night I got into trouble for the third time is again, a blur. I caused some property damage and started a fire if my memory serves me correctly. I insulted one of my friend's girlfriend and made a shitshow of myself to everyone that was there. The cops were called and my First Sergeant showed up to pick me up and take me to base. It was one or two in the morning I think. I woke up in the Duty bedroom. I knew   I was in trouble. I walked back to my barracks room shortly after talking with higher ups. I wasn't sure what was going to happen, but I had a feeling my time in the Marine Corps was up. I was placed on a sixty day restriction and NJP'd. That is a term which stands for Non-Judicial Punishment. The military has its own justice system. Once you get punished by local authority, the Marine Corps also can punish you if the crime is severe enough. I was docked pay and demoted to private first class. Rock bottom has a lot of layers and rooms to it. I learned it all the hard way and I am still forgiving myself because of it. The day It took almost two months for me to be discharged from the Corps. In that time, I had a few more drinking episodes, stopped giving a fuck about everything. Since my Battalion had deployed, the holdovers, including myself, were sent to a different one. We weren't training anymore. We simply woke up for roll-call at five or six in the morning, then went back to bed and did whatever we wanted to for the most part. I began sending boxes of my belongings home to my dad's house. I was out of shape and out of my right mind in so many ways. the day came to leave and I had never felt more less of a human in my life. I basically left the same way I arrived to boot camp, lost and a shell of who I had been before. The plane ride was unnerving. The waiting was unnerving. Everything about the day and what would come was fucking ruthless to who I thought I had become. I don't blame anyone or anything for my demise. It all started and ended with me and I made the worst judgment calls when it came to believing I knew myself. It turned out when I got back from war, it wasn't me who returned. It was a hollowed out version of the man I fought to keep alive years before joining the Marines. There is never a day that goes by when I don't have a flashback and wish I had the courage to step away form alcohol for good and never go back to the house where everything truly changed my course. I know everyone has that one or singular moment they can snap back into and know if they had done just one thing differently, it would all be better. Or that is what we tell ourselves to justify what we are currently feeling. I went to college the first time as a student who was going to major in psychology. I knew if they only had classes on it itself, I would have stayed in. There was something intriguingly made by the thought of figuring out the human mind and psyche. It is what most fascinates me besides the universe itself. I do my best not to regret anything I have done because it would mean I wouldn't be here, right now, typing this out and making another book for someone else to read. I hope by the end of it, you come closer to who you need to be, who you are looking to become in the whole finite picture of what you see when you gaze out upon the moon and sun. We are all in this for some reason, this incredulous rat race where there is no winner, only empty truths we must rinse out and fill with our own.

Chapter VI

-POETRY-

i know one day this will end. this extreme suffering for a love i'll never have. i do my best with these empty spots within me. they make up a large portion of my sacrifices without gaining anything back besides more words on paper for someone to read. i can only hope others find a way to connect to them, because once i let them go, they no longer belong to me. every writing i've ever done, is a child i learned to love as it is were my own blood. they are conceived by a darkness and light marrying together, for better or worse, until their death gives life to what remains.

what you want, what you are in need of may cost you everything, but only convicted truth will get you there. who you are, every version of who you have been, all of these manifestations of survival will need to be released. this alignment you seek, mind, body, soul, will hold space for you until you create space for the change itself.

we were high as stars that night, getting lost in love at first sight. maybe the moon had us in our feelings, seeking both sides of the road to keep what we felt separated by what we didn't know. the year had been a harsh one for us both. we had to learn how to console parts of ourselves no one else wanted to hold. they say misery loves company, but it didn't want any part of me. you became an oath to me, strong as oak with roots as deep as sea. we were one with the gods that night. it made the devil laugh, knowing there was no darkness left to divide lovers unafraid to die and ready for the ride only open highways provide.

i know there will be an untold story about you and i. one we will only know. one where winter turned to gold and sat with spring to make sure may had her flowers. i've been out on the limbs again, while the birds keep my longing company. a pain like this, deeply embedded inside this aching chest, should've killed me by now. but these feathered friends of mine continue to sing with shine which makes love rise with bright eyes and a sonder smile. withing this affection i carry for you, i'll never forget what life was like when i took every chance i had to look at you as if i already knew what missing you was going to be for me. time doesn't heal anything, it only shows us how long it's been since we were happy, how long it's been since our hearts had been broken.

love will always be the calming of chaos which you have done for me. you may not have been aware of the hurricane in me, but i knew the gentle breeze within you. i am not only my greatest self with you, i know what you've given to me, no one else ever could. my fire is because of you. each flame and color is a representation of your soul dancing with mine. everyone doesn't understand how many times you actually have to die to find what keeps you alive, what keeps you going when the rest of the world gave up trying. you have shown me rest, a dedicated pause of reflection. my madness knows peace because i know your name. in life, we will suffer greatly for the wrong things. this life with you, will always be the first thing i tell someone when they ask me what happy feels like, what it looks like before you became unbroken. you are my healing.

she gave all she had.
when others ask her where she gets her strength from, she takes a breath, then points to her moon. every day the battle seems to find her. her fight has been tested before by those who could not come close to her giving spirit. there are still those who bet against her with their own lives and end up losing more than they'd ever imagined. she is not from the same energy as you. she resides in spaces of a broken heart still trying to find where it belongs. if you want to help her, don't approach her with your own ideas of who you want her to be. come with love, and only love. her dreams are too precious to be tamed by hardened humans, by a light unrequited. if you are seeking refuge, she is not for you. she holds the universe in her eyes, an all consuming force of beauty and hell. you do not know her like i do. all women are held to a certain standard, a set of rules they are made to obey. not this one. you'll never see her again once you ask her to change for the sake of making things easier for you, for the life you believe you're helping by altering who she's always been before you thought she needed saving.

there are a million places staged by a thousand faces. each one filled with blood forged by a hundred moons and ten dying suns. i am the outsider to this land. it is behind the curtains where i am reciting hamlet and all the faults are mine, not the stars. becoming this version of bone and flesh took years of practice and postponed abilities to let go of a past that was never mine to begin with. maybe in another life, love won't feel as though you are losing your mind, instead of gaining a heart to bleed with. lovely souls call out to me. take me from your prayer and add me to a list of sinners with tattoos to show proof of my existence, to show i actually lived.

through the fire you walked out. flames could never tame you. ashes, you are not. where you are going, it will take all of your power, your glory, your magic, to endure what has killed many, but not you. the life you have lived up until now, was a testament to the broken you have been harboring. you've become a thousand versions of someone you once needed long ago in the shadows of a world you never fit into. your grace is a portrait of colors and emotions wrapped in hope and adventure. may you always find the light that feeds you, that fans the fever you've been born with. i know now not all mountains have a name, but yours do. each climb, each fall, every attempt became a story written all over your face. you are the good in goodbye, and nothing will come close to destroying your rise.

do not be afraid of your gifts, dear child. not everyone will understand you or care to know you. you are the blessing of all the suns and moons. you've always been capable of flying. you simply need to trust your wings for the first time. being a feeler of energy and light, you'll need to accept yourself first before anyone else will. there is no such thing as a curse. this breath you are breathing, found you and gave you life. being different is the most magical thing that can happen to an individual. the way we see the world, brings out the stars even during the day. you are an ocean, a cosmic inclusion, a display of what can become of those who are born to be a gift to those in need of a miracle. shine on, bright light. shine on.

when the moon comes to rescue the stars, it takes its cue from you. there are humans who become a shelter, a well defined landscape of light and magic. you've been one since the day your light was given a name. it's been seen and adored for a million years, for cities and countries deprived of love. many have traveled to find such a thing, but you've always been home for the lost, the broken, the lonely. many will never make it to you, but your power lies within the miles you trek to locate them, first. it is why you were made of flowers and poetry.

i can't tell anyone that i love you. it hurts to speak to you knowing i'll never be anything more than a distraction for you, someone that passes the time. i used to think talking about how you felt for another was the easiest way to declare a love. now i know it's only a goodbye that slows down the rest of your life. i used to think it was my fault when love wasn't reciprocated. i understand now how much of ourselves will never be accepted, because we have yet to accept our own trauma that made us feel guilty for feeling hopeful about anything at all.

maybe someday when we are older, we will look back and remember these as good times, a fullness almost forgotten. i know nothing escapes the fray, not even love we have made and kept safe from the grave. i want to believe in a place where we make it. i want to believe in you, in us, in anything getting us closer to tomorrow, instead of another yesterday where our togetherness was a strangeness to the strangers in us.

i'm not even sure i want love these days. it's a feeling many do not know how to convey. i sit here hopelessly rotting away, eating parts of my tongue to stay silent and fed until the next time hunger reminds me of you. there was a time when you would tell me about the life you wanted. in that version, i was a part of it. i've tried to give what's left of me to a few others over the years, but no one knows what they want. i'll go back to the wolves for now. at least they know what they are howling for. at least they are starving for everything.

you've always been the way for me, the love for me, the feeling of completed harmony. you're the wings to my body, the reason why humans feel connected to my words. without you, i'm nameless, faceless, another bird singing for a sunrise from a deadwood tree. i only mourn you in the morning, then i do my best to love your absence throughout my day. being away from you has taught me how much you can miss someone's voice, when their face leaves your memory.

there are parts of me too dark for this place, so i write about them to ease my own suffering. we are   all artists, whether by choice or what someone has done to us. some paint, write, draw, drink, or self-destruct. only a few know how to love and be loved. the rest of us are moved by songs we cannot sing, but we dance to them as if it is good enough for the moment we are in. i'm somewhere in the middle, learning how to be alone again and not hold in my breath.

some days i have no words, a true empty space between my heart and mind. on those days it is still a beautiful fight. it remains the only way for me to know my human side. not always being okay, is okay. i need you to never forget that when you feel out of place, when you forget your own face. to know your pain on an intimate level, is how our cracks and breaks turn golden.

there's something deeply felt about her. in the way her hair falls just to the right, when all other living things fall left. not everyone will get to know her as the moon does, and that's why love gravitates towards her. it's why nothing else makes sense if you do not know of her. beauty is a fine line once the bones begin to break for lies, for the abstract contours of innocence and sorrow. a blessing is only that if you have known to be cursed. a gentle wave becomes a maverick after ripping out the heart of the sea. if you wish to do the same thing to her, she will hold your soul down and drown everything you've become. she's all truth, all war, all undefined magic, existing in a far too materialistic world.

only in october do i feel loved. it's a season unlike any other. holy spirits and ghostly encounters are the only things that can keep my love down and my heart upright. if you sway like this any longer, the trees we leave for groundly meetings will forever set us up with a lover's greeting. i wish i didn't have to hide all my faces. each mask covering shades of erased phases of who i have had to let go in order to become myself, to find you, to be here now with uncertainty painting goodbyes before they are said. october is a cruel beauty, which leaves you lingering, barely able to make it to november, until it is gone again. nothing remains but the trees; empty and without proof of life to show for its sacrifices.

a separated hallelujah saved from all the wreckage. it's always going to be you who i hope to hold. i'll be the only one remaining with a lantern looking for the parts you left behind for me to find of you. there is not enough light, not enough fire, not enough openness in this world to ever get close to you again. i could try and spill more blood to do so, but taking on devils and demons is a past life of mine i let go of when you left me for the first time.

prepare yourself for war. not to kill, but to be understood. from wings made of colors we both have shared. the purpose means nothing without steady work and sacrifice. to be captured by you, will be my greatest victory within defeat. it is how i will know my name when someone asks me next time. it is how my eyes will now shine when i find a sun and moon too good to be alive in this world. i am a lunatic when it comes to the ordinary parts of earth itself. give me a hand and i will show you how to lead with poetry, instead of whatever else you have learned to be love.

maybe there will be more trees for us down the road. to hold you for that brief moment in time, gave my heart a timely sigh, a suspended belief that we will work out and come across a life together. you said you would look like someone who just murdered someone else. you looked like a woman i'd give all of my words to. you looked like summer as i remembered that time of year when i was a child of sin and despair. you are every golden flake of sun and every infant bloom grasping to its light. if i see you again, if i get to love you once more, i'm going to the other side with you. you gave me hope that eyes can still find me in the dark. you gave me hands instead of the rope others handed to me when i told them i needed help. you never forget who god turns out to be for you in this life.

you never wanted to leave neverland, but i wasn't peter pan. i was just another lost boy looking for love and a hand to hold to get me home. looking at you now, i know the moon has taught you well. the wolves might have raised you, but she will always be your mother, daughter of light. so tonight, just know i am holding on as tight as i can. as far as holding goes, your closeness is the heart of every body that has been abandoned by the lonely. you are the silent prayer of all my sins, my lovely.

there's a price for everything. if you want it, you will have to break a little, bleed a little, die a little. you will have to scream and call it out by name. a heart on the sleeve is the only way to love. it is the only way to properly fight off anything not meant for you. the blindfold they use on the eyes, will be removed as soon as they raise their weapons to end my life. once i am free at last, i will come to look for your brown and hazel eyes. one thing you will need to know, is if you remain staring at the sea as you do so lovingly, your colors will turn to blue and my love for you will be lost at the bottom of it all. you've become my obsession, my next adventure to take. if i ever get a full day with you, i can only hope to hold you for its duration. my heart is yours for the breaking should it ever come to that.

there was always something different about her. something beautifully unnoticed by most. you never really knew how much she was suffering. a quietness rested beneath her struggles, but she still persisted, she still found a way to be mighty, even as her tiny hands fought off more than anyone ever saw. today is the day she almost died for. she's free now; free to love, free to fly.

love never meant much to me growing up. seeing my parents sleep in separate rooms after arguing and going to sleep without telling each other, i love you. it is something that sticks with me to this day. love to me, is carrying the soul of another, caring for their heart when a closeness is what you're after. when it is the only thing that will give you peace within dreams and a reality you awaken to.

the love i have for you, keeps the moon full of your precious light. wherever you are from, beauty was defined by it. take my bones with you. take my soul with you. take me in every place you feel lonely. take me wherever you go in this world. i will never love anything more than seeing this place through your eyes, your movements, your requited approach to being who you are, when there was a time in your life you never thought you belonged to it.

i wanted you to remember how it felt to be loved, to be wanted, to be missed. too often we go without what we need because we don't ask for it or we are with the wrong love. i hope you speak about the life you want. i hope your beauty never goes out of style. i hope you shine on. may we only ever go crazy for the madness to heal our hearts and matches our own. may these words always find you before the sun does.

you've become the inhale, the exhale, the breath of a warrior. there aren't many who could keep going with as many wounds as you've collected. but here you are, fighting off demons and dragons, becoming the one we all look to for saving. love becomes the essence of who we are once the heart begins to become aware of its power and magnitude. each one is different, and that is why we will never agree on what love actually is. but when it comes to you, there is no mistaking the ability you were born with to make others feel their own.

my greatest strength has always been you. you have given me a newly found purpose, an incredible shift from man to soul. your love gave my life reason to speak. i'll never get enough of this feeling of you. fly with wings made of bravery, gold, and truth. fly with a blazing sun, flames and flares fanning out beyond the names of gods and devils.

take me down to your river. lead me away from temptation, away from the absence my hands currently hold. make me no promises. tell me how this goes. wake me up with your touch forever and always. we hope there is something beyond this day that will keep us from becoming who we have already been before. we hope there is another heart we can share this with when it comes to finding a human who feels too familiar to let go of.

you know me so well, just as the moon knows my own darkness. her light keeps all of me in the safety of her arms. there's human love, then there is hers. love is something i am still learning, still trying to decide if i am good at it or not. i am unsure if it will stay for me. i have known it for all my life, but maybe i am too old to believe in something good happening for me for the sake of my intentions. maybe i am just enough for myself now and no one else. maybe my teacher has always been loss and learning what good enough is, is simply a perspective only we can use.

i'm still exploring for the right feeling, the right sensation, the right everything. i've been told there's no such thing, but you once gave it all to me. maybe it only comes around once in a single lifetime. i guess loving again will decide if it's all worth it. i oftentimes imagine us together in every place we once talked about. i know you are going to be his wife at some point this year. i guess when half of your heart leaves, memories take its place. it seems to be all i have these days of anything or anyone i have ever cared about.

maybe love has a name like yours and a face carved out of every mountain you've carried and conquered. maybe love is softer than the texture of flesh and rugged as the brokenness we are all made of. maybe if we give bravery a try, everything else will fall into place. maybe our arms can hold onto it next time. it hasn't been easy trying to find the correct path, a decent descent to a place where you feel needed and are accepted. i have been there once before. destroy your comfort zones. all of them. only the dead can say anything good about them.

she never knew where to go, but she always ended up leaning against the wind. a softly made rain drop, she lands where she's needed. love is her name. i'm still clinging to the thought of you, to the light of you, to the idea our love will survive the chaos we've danced with. my soul is only yours to move. my life is only yours when you need it to be more than a phone call or message to check and see if i will reply. you and i have already lived a lifetime together from a distance. i am holding out hope for one more to find us either in this extreme or somewhere on the other side.

in my head, it all worked out. all the smiles when you were near, my face has forgotten how to make love appear where you placed it. my eyes sag below the life i am living. my movements are nothing more than hesitation and pause. i am lost to this lifeless cause of breathing in nothing that matters but the art that comes from your absence. you got engaged three days ago. i remember you told me you would never marry again. it didn't crush me, because i knew all along you would run back to him at some point. it is what those who need safety and security do. i am not talking about physical security. i knew i would never be able to get you a house on the beach, a life made easy by having every means to never fear being without luxuries. i do not apologize for that. you and i both knew what we wanted. time changes everything, especially when an old flame never burns out and comes back to burn down what you were trying to make. our house would had never been safe from it all. i am just thankful you left when you did and didn't leave me in there to die alone.

love will always feel like an early morning, full of birds singing and their wings keeping hearts safe and in place amongst their actions. i hope this life becomes an immortal sun for you. i hope this life shows you a justified moon, set out to shine their truthful light upon your journey. may you never lose your freedom. may your bravery be the blood.

take me down to the song of your soul. give me one last kiss, one last touch, one last dance. my feet have only known this mumbled earth below me. i am in need of your chaos to rattle these caged bones of mine. love will always be enough. even on days when that is all you have. some fail to see the beauty of letting go the fear. it is the act itself when magic happens and you are left in wonderment, with a smile stretched from sea to sky.

you became my first wish of the new year. i will call out our name each time i see one of my angel numbers. i may never be any closer to than this, but you need to know how much of my breath is already yours. you need to know the home inside me, the one you had built before this life, misses you. i keep looking out its windows in hopes you are running back to me, to us. if it take being alone with my demons and you with your new love, i shall wait out both heaven and hell to have you as you've always been to me; something holy and wholly only for me. my lord. my god, i am defeated by your beauty. i am nesting in a sunset until i can hold you in all of your glory.

i don't know how to live without you,
to love if it isn't you. i wander
these streets at night, hoping to catch
your reflection in the disregarded
light. i am a master of nothing, but
mastering a life full of your absence.
it is the one thing i will need to
perfect if i am ever going to hold a
new warmth again. i am not really
sure where it all goes when all of this
is over, but i will want you always,
in the same way a permanent
moon never leaves the sun's side
or any star left dangling, hanging
on by the light of you.

become the lion and go about your life. it is too short to be around those who feed off of you, instead of helping you hunt. fall in love with the journey, not the destination. all too often we break ourselves for nothing more than an ending we could have avoided. once you see who you fucking are, you will never accept anyone's leftovers. you will never sit at a table not serving you. you are the myth of every story the gods once talked about when it came to the fields of gold, to the warrior who could never die or be defeated by anyone claiming to be your equivalent in any way. your sword still drips of dark red and sunset. you once cut the sky from top to bottom just to show someone there is no lie in you.

i don't want to look back on my life and wish i had given more. i want to exhaust every breath and moment of the journey i am on. i don't want to waste who i am on those that ask for more of me when they barely give me their eyes when i speak their name. i am not here to live the same day for fifty years. i am not here for anything resembling ordinary. i do not want nonchalant or excuses for failing to give me what i deserve, from me or anyone. i know i am emotional, strange, and intense, but at least i know who i fucking am. at least i know what i fucking want. the dead parts inside of me are coming back to life. i will not die again to be someone else's backup. if you cannot give me honesty, i cannot give you truths. i am me. all i ask is for you to be, you, with me. all i ask from you is to raise the stars together, as we live on through each night. some days i feel as if i am at war with myself, my own bloody thoughts. i am not sure if it is a single voice or many, but it does a number on me. people ask me what anxiety feels like. i cannot speak for others, but for me, it is basically me thinking i am going to die that second. it replays on a loop, a consistent act of betrayal of my own doing. it can last all day or only come in spurts. i say this not for your sympathy, but to let others know you are not alone if it happens to you. at the end of the day. i am still alive and my mind rests. there's victory in everything we go through. surviving my own anxious episodes is one for me. if we choose to suffer in silence, we will deprive ourselves from anything looking like help, like love, like a hand to hold to keep us grounded.

i keep your memory close to me and wear it like a favorite blanket. i look up to the moon to not only feel you, but to remember where you are when my mind blinds my ability to see clearly. i can remain still for hours, and i'd still feel the steps you make without me being there next to you. you are such a force, a choir of magic, an hourglass that never completely runs out of time. you are my arms, legs, hands, and feet. where i go, our bodies will always meet. you are the single mermaid of my waters, a deeply haunting wave i can never escape. i will never give up trying to get you back, even now without you, i have your goodbye in my back pocket. whenever your heart is waging war against your mind, i will give my sword to you and i will be your shield. when i said forever, i meant in every life, in every breath beyond being human.

Chapter VII

-INWARDLY-

I wish I could tell you it gets easier, that somehow everything you are going through will change you for the better. Sometimes it is only in the brief moment itself we find what we are looking for, then we lose it all again. It took me decades to figure this out. But with all of the chaos that found me eventually, I learned to appreciate it all. I learned how to adapt to what was happening more so than I did before when I just went with the flow. Traveling around the states, I picked up a lot of new feelings and emotions. I acquired new tastes for music, food, and even energies from those I came into contact with. Growing up, I honestly did my best to hide within the crowds, to not make any noise. I was afraid of being the center of attention, which is still how I am today. I do not go out looking for appreciation, for applause, for recognition of any kind. I am happiest when it is just me and my own thoughts. I have stayed in roach motels for thirty dollars a night. They all smelt of dried out cigarettes and rummaging around in the open air without washing it off of you. I didn't mind it, because I knew you got what you paid for. It was easier for me to spend less on a room so I could spend my money in other areas of my trips. I've also stayed in hundred dollar rooms, but never a penthouse. I've stayed in suites, in camp sites with the stars for a blanket. I've slept in my truck a few times, but that was back when I was young enough to wake up still hungover and feeling as though some coffee and breakfast would do the trick. Obviously I am not as young as I once was, and that has kept me from doing certain things simply out of knowledge for knowing who I am now. Expectations once got the best of me. They once corroded my insides and turned me into a shell of who I was before I thought it was something I needed to do and become. Meeting new people is a beautiful blessing. Strangers are my favorite kind of human. They don't know a single thing about you. They can only judge you for a brief moment before they end up trusting you to carry on a conversation or leave you without anything to speak of. Either way, the encounter alone gives me more experience with who I am. They taught me so much as a young kid and in my adolescent years. Elderly humans are another favorite of mine. All they want is someone to talk to for the most part. They probably have spent the last several years of their lives seeking connections and someone who cares, if only for the time you are around them. I love listening to their stories.

I love knowing they find me comforting and familiar enough to unleash whatever it is they have to give for that day. My grandparents were like that. I only have one grandmother left who is in her nineties, but still as spry as any child looking to do what needs to be done. They were one of the most stable moments of my early life. As the years went on and I went through my teenage phase, I appreciated them even more, even if they didn't always agree with what I dressed like or looked like as I developed through the music I listened to and had alcohol and drugs in my life. There is no love like the love from them. I was in the hospital room the day my grandfather took his last breath. The scream from my mother still echoes through me. My grandmother laid beside him, corralling him as though he was nothing more than injured. The gasp of air that came out of his mouth filled the entire room around us. I could feel his spirit leave his body. It is a moment that changed me like all deaths do I suppose. It wasn't my first time witnessing someone die, but it was one of the first times it was one of my own family members. Throughout my life, death has known me better than most living things. In some ways, I felt connected to it at an early age. We moved all over the country for a long time. Somewhere between thirty and forty times to be exact. I found myself in a few haunted houses that could have made a brilliant horror film. Fireplaces going up in flames by themselves, crying babies in my brother's room. My action figures flying on their own. Seeing ghosts and them going through me as I laid there in my bed, frozen and fearful of the red eyes I saw. Being connected to energy causes you to become more in-tune with yourself, with who you are as a human. Being an empath is something I never understood until I realized it was responsible for my drinking and drug use as a teenager and into my early twenties. I value it more than I ever did before. I was in a relationship several years ago and she was the one who really taught me about it. She understood me like no other ever has. If I felt something, I told her and she would give me an honest reply if I was correct or if I was making up the feeling to satisfy my mood. Knowing you have someone who isn't trying to sabotage you is one of the greatest comforts there is in this world. I'm not always sure or confident in my gifts. They take a lot out of me, right or wrong. The journey is a never-ending attempt at correcting your posture to fit with the soul you carry. Every day won't be the same as the one before. It is why we must do all we can to make room for new experiences and new encounters. Those are the things that shape us completely. They form the exoskeleton inside of us. Today has been another scorcher. The heat index was near one hundred and fifteen or so. All blue sky. All sun and burnt grass. I actually had to mow today. My dad waters the lawn every other day just so we don't have a dead yard like the rest of the neighborhood. he enjoys being outside more than most. it stems from how he grew up and being around his father. He will be sixty-nine in a few months. He got a haircut yesterday for the first time this year. He likes having longer hair these days,　but the heat was getting to him. I hope to get a vacation in some time during the end of summer. I am not sure where to yet, but I know I need to get away.

Being stagnate isn't something I am good at. Though I have developed into accepting I won't always be able to go places and do what I want to do being here, and that's okay. There really isn't nothing like saving money during a pandemic. Gas prices seem to be leveling off a bit. They have gone down to three dollars and eighty-six cents. A few days ago it was over four. It's making it more manageable to hopefully start making plans to go on the next adventure. I miss it dearly. I am not the same human if I am not able to get on the road and stay away for a few weeks here and there. Recharging and resetting the energy is a necessary mission for me. To remain balanced and happy and not invite negativity into my world is a priority for me. Keeping up with my mental health is just as important to me as maintaining my sobriety. The two go hand in hand, almost a marriage of sorts. Each day I do my best to provide myself a better future, a more promising beginning to a new sensation of knowing I am getting closer to making those dreams a reality. Some days I wish it all away in an attempt to get there sooner. Being patient is something I am extremely good at, probably too good. It's gotten the best of me on several occasions. Waiting too long for something to happen or waiting just enough to ruin it all. Being stuck so to speak, in the same place for years on end will do that to you. I do not wish it on anyone. It feels like you are being held captive in your own world with a way out, yet you choose to remain with the suffering, as if it is there for you in a loving manner. To make sense of it all, I write, or at least try to get it all out of my system so the next day can have more potential to lead me down a more openly chiseled path. Obstructions will always be there. It's all about understanding why they are there. Road blocks and set backs are a part of life. Not all of them are meant to dissuade you or put you into a more dire state of living. You must clear out the path yourself if you are to find what has been hiding in plain sight. Love is like that, too. I've known it to be the moon, along with it becoming a hellish rendition of life meeting death in its infant stages. My muses have all been stretched out for the universe to see, but I have kept the names from the public. They will never be known. For a writer, they are your special ingredient, the magic that makes humans attracted to it in the first place. if they can see themselves within your words, they are there forever, or until they no longer feel as though it is who they are anymore. I am thankful for those who discover my work. It is still insane to me that I have a career made out of my thoughts and emotions. How beautiful it is to remain inspired by life and give back to it by giving yourself the life you have dreamt about since the child you were who learned how to be themselves unapologetically. This world really is a wondrous landscape. In the same breath, it is the prison as well for a lot of us who cannot escape our minds and inabilities to process them. I wish it were easier for so many who struggle. I feel it all anyway, so to know those who connect to my words, I know personally the fight they are enduring. It is a brave thing to show yourself to it, to make it known how much of it actually isn't conducive for you and the life you are searching for. To be an artist, you openly discuss or showcase your trauma, which brings it back to you. Somehow, the healing exists there, too. Opening a wound. Closing a wound. It is how we breathe. It is how we speak. It is how we love. It is how we'll die. There is no better therapy than finding it with your creative side. it is a switch that never turns off. The levee full to the brim, but rain still pours down, breaching our bones, then destroying us all over again. Rinse. Recycle. Repeat. It is as simple and chaotic as that. Writing this now, I have felt every feeling I ever had as a child. The images. The sounds. The silence. all of it incubated my premature emotional integrity. Nothing feels as good as letting it all out and sifting through the mud to find your gold, the lotus which never dies. Writing is a gift I never took full advantage of until almost ten years ago. I knew it would always be there for me should I need it. I wasn't prepared for it becoming my life's work. Now, it is here with me. I love and console it daily. I cherish each writing of mine as if it were my own child, knowing I won't ever have any. They are nameless, yet I know who they belong to and why. Many days I find myself struggling with it all. The monotony of life, the slowness of breaths too afraid to risk something for what is needed. There are too many dying souls in these streets. The ones walking without purpose, without reason as to why they are going in the direction to begin with. I do not want to be one of them. I do not want to bring down who I am to meet them where they have stayed and remained stuck their entire lives. I can smell death when they are near me. I can see the gravestones in their eyes. I cannot stand be around normalcy, around anything resembling it.

It dampens my fire and turns me off completely to the notion that something more is out there based on what these nomads haven't found. Please do not waste my time when you approach me with a thought. Please do not call my name out loud if you are to whisper stupidity or nothing into my ear. I will not fall for your antics. I have only played it safe a few times. And in those times, I have failed miserably. I wasn't able to open up to the sun above me and the moon right next to the stars. My failures have taught me more than my victories. I believe that is how life is supposed to be. I believe it is the only time we figure out who we are during the battle and after the sacrifice. Looking outwardly, I notice the entire world changing right in front of me. The outspoken continue to rant and rave about some agenda they have. Others think they are

Gods or some embodiment of Christ himself with the way they want to be worshiped. I'm sure their crosses are heavier than yours or mine. I'm sure their thorns have been worn this entire time, even when they came out of the womb. I don't understand humanity. I honestly don't think I ever will. I hope I never do. There isn't anything I want them to teach me. Lessons of life only serve me when I am living it, not being told what it was once like. Conflicted and fictitious feelings invade my lands. Congruently measured hearts keep most of us out of the dark, out of the loop from ever belonging to a greater cause than ourselves. Walking around the towns and cities I've found myself in, you notice the intricacies of what separates us from the next. You notice how a lady sips her drink or how a man holds his woman tightly to his chest or at arm's length.

You notice the sounds someone makes when they enjoy a memorable meal or a moment surrounded by their loved ones. You notice the child in the corner of the room, cut-off from his family and chastised for being young. You notice how the light finds the love in the room. You become immersed in these precarious but beautiful moments when a human erupts into flowers or sits quietly watching everyone else die in front of him or her. The dance is never over. The song never skips. The feet never tire. The hands always wander. The eyes always figure out how to lie, but still speak of truth. You learn how everyone around you is someone you never knew of before. You begin to realize how many of us are actually living parallel lives, where intersected parts of it become a story untold. You may feel too overwhelmed to even begin to fathom how incredibly large this stage is we are on. The mouth begins to vibrate. The hands begin to shake. The body begins to sway back and forth. You are alive. You are aware of infinities, and I hope you never settle for less than at least one of those in every moment that catches you off guard and empty handed. Randomness best describes me and what I do. Though I am able to maintain my focus long enough to get through what it is I am trying to get done. I believe some of us are better off not abiding by the rules and going off-script. My entire life has been one fire after another. Throwing more paper, more love, more bones, more of myself into it all for the sake of making ends meet. If you never venture out beyond the city limits of your own town, you will be on your way to pick out your own burial plot not long after you decide that's what's best for you. I'll never shit on someone who is conflicted about what they should do. At the end of the day, we are the only ones who know what is best for us. But I will make sure I get my point across beforehand to let them know and show them what happens to those who never feel the fire of a raging sun. Those who never get close enough to the moon to kiss her scars. Those who never got across the state line and into territory they never knew existed. That's what I am alive for. That's what keeps me going. The unknown out there. The words awaiting for me on my arrival. The newly found emotions that will set in and drive me to the next destination while I am riding shotgun. These last few years have made us all a bit stir crazy. In the same breath, it has turned some of us into humans who will never go anywhere again. I hope fear doesn't hold you back. I hope the idea of death doesn't scare you away from living. We must remember from time to time that we will die, that right now is all we have to live for. To earn a full life, you will need to give a full life in return. This is non-negotiable. There is only one way to live, and that is to give your all to a purpose, for a cause. Never sell yourself short in anyway. Speaking it out loud is the same as someone else saying it to you and you believing it to be true. It is something I'm still working on. All of my life, I have had moments of doubt and self-loathing. it isn't sustainable if you want something that will stay. We lose ourselves before we ever find anything else to give ourselves to. When it came to my purpose, I knew it would be writing. I honestly don't know why it took me as long as it did to believe it for myself. I would write every day at times. I've thrown away more pages than most will ever write in their lifetime. Not everything we create, be it any form of art, will be our best, but it is crucial to hold it close regardless. The steps taken to get to where we are today were earned. Nothing in my life has ever been given to me. I've fought since I took my first breath and I will go out the same way, with sword and shield in hand, standing on mountains made of my progress, my goals, my dreams. It's been a long fucking road for me personally. There hasn't been anything that hasn't tried to kill me or pull me away and off course. I've gone entirely mad from the battles, from the drink, from anything or anyone who has shown me comfort. I know I am fully faulted. My heart has been the most bruised part about me.

My scars are not only an ongoing saga, they are my novels, a personal tale of triumphing evil lurking inside and outside of me. There will be more difficult days before good ones learn to stay around me. Speaking gently, I lift encouragement to everyone who struggles with self, with demons, with assurance. We are here for a reason. A breath will fight on forever if given a chance to. Breathe in deeply the feelings you seek, the life you want, and anything that makes you feel whole. Too often we fall by the wayside in order to appease the general public to let them know we mean them no harm. I am not one of those. Though I don't mean anyone harm, I will fight off anyone who is looking to cause me the same. I was born a warrior, full of determination and skill to succeed in anything I put my mind to. I haven't always given it my full attention, but in the end, I came out victorious because of my mindset. I am neither half-full or half-empty. I have everything I need and then some based on what I have given back, knowing I'd get nothing back in return. Being able to be comfortable in an uncomfortable world gets you further in any walk of life. Today is one of those days I give myself to rest, to soak in the light a bit more. Sunday for me is not a church full of humans either demanding some form of truth or some kind of lie to feel better about what they did wrong for a week, or who they fucked or fucked over during the same times frame. For me, it is typing away, making sure the sun stays in the corner of my room to watch me work. It is feeling each word walk across my arms and fall off my tongue. Silence suits me well in most cases. I do not need to talk to someone else to feel heard or feel seen. I am in the midst of my greatest achievements. I am the student and teacher of these halls. I have nothing, but in my nothingness, the gold is mine to have, to share. I find love to be near me even when I have none to hold. I find love in the images in my head of what it was once like to tell someone, thank you for loving me. There are humans who inflict pain upon us because they've been without comfort, without knowledge of what it takes to be human. I don't feel sorry for them. Some of us only know destruction, because starvation leads us to be that way. There will be a full moon tonight. It is called a Buck Moon, and it will be a super moon. Supposedly, it will be the closest and brightest one of the year. I haven't really looked at the moon in a long time. Not like I used to anyway. It's what happens when you turn things and objects into humans, into muses. The inanimate objects we pull our inspiration from become something grander because of our love for someone. Now, I cannot look at it without thinking of her. What a waste of power I have given away. I occasionally find myself putting my thumb over it as Tom Hanks did in Apollo 13. He did it as a reminder to himself of how small we are in this life. Of how minuscule we all are down here. Ants marching towards the sun. Birds flying into the abyss of darkness. Humans arguing over the smallest of things when in the end, nothing truly fucking matters as much as what you feel, need, and live for. The purpose behind the drive inside. The subtle nudge you get randomly one day as a sensation encompasses you and brings you to your fucking knees in a state of being overwhelmed. We tend to give ourselves to things that will never fully appreciate who we are and what we have to give because it is who we are. Change is possible, of course, but when it comes to the fibers and fabrics of our soul, nothing will stop us from showing the love we will probably die not ever knowing. I am okay with it. I always have been. I knew it would be the case for the longest.   Though I did find it when I found her. She couldn't give herself completely because of the situation she found herself in, but it was more than anyone had ever given before. Even with the distance between our breaths, my lungs were full and healing for the firs time. I had never felt love like that. I had never had someone speak to me in a way that was both comforting and direct, without being condescending. Some of us need a bit extra. Be it love, care, conversation, walking aimlessly or driving off and forgetting about life for a while. The search remaining is not a destination, but a feeling, an event not of this world. We want to believe in something having meaning and it being ours. We want to believe there is reason and meaning behind our aches, and not just some bullshit excuse from someone saying they are sorry for hurting us again. We hurt ourselves more times than not. I know I have personally. My mind gets twisted up and knotted several times a day. I do my best to untangle it to understand why I am feeling it and why I am here suffering. The full moon tonight will be a lovely welcome for a new beginning of sorts. It doesn't always have to be a full moon to feel deeply or more intensely than any other day, but it is a giant redirect of all things living. A counter-balance some of us believe in. Knowing what I know now, it will be opening up an old wound, though we must if we are ever to move on from it. We must strike the depths of who we are with all the magic and truth we can to reinforce the structure we were made to be. My philosophy has changed a million times over the course of my life. I used to believe in a single God and go to church and lead youth camps for a small time. Then I grew to understand what it meant to not be religious and have spirituality become who you are. I've given all I have to my craft, both inside and out. I do not care for those who wish me to be unsuccessful or harm. I do not care for those who cannot see my dreams or desires. I simply live for my own doing, however selfish you may think it is. It is what it takes if you want the life you want. You eventually grow out of it and open yourself up to someone else being in your life. I ask you not to name things after objects. The hurt lingers for years, because a lot of it you cannot destroy. For a star is already dying, but its light is a reminder of who it was and your old love will be the same. You are not the same human when you enter into a new relationship. If you are, you are already doing yourself and the one you are with a disservice. If you did not learn anything from a past relationship, your growth is forever singular and nothing new ever comes from remaining the same year in, year out, love in and love out. I went to the dentist the other day. Dr. Brady's dentistry is in Southlake, which is about six hours or more from where I live. Last year on Veteran's day, I made a video of my insecurity, which was my smile. Someone had messaged him asking if he could help me with it. Something I didn't even know about nor did I make the video for that reason. Dr. Brady messaged me a little bit after I had posted it. I thought I was getting scammed by some ghost account, but it was real. He asked me to come in for a consultation and he would pay for my dental treatment. I probably cried for a few days. I had never had someone help me like that before. I've always been the one who was the giver, the helper. I couldn't believe my good fortune was finally coming to fruition. I say that to say this, good things happen to good people. In the same breath, they also happen to the worst of us, but I had never felt as much joy and being seen as that moment gave to me. A year plus later and I finished my Invisalign treatment. Not all of my teeth are straight, but I have the smile I never had before. A lot of the time I still close lip smile, because I forget I have a new one to show. It is simply out of habit for doing it for over thirty plus years. We never know when our life will change for the better or for worse for that matter. We only have control over this day, and this day only. Whatever comes to you, I hope you are prepared to handle it in whatever way you can. I hope you have the means and fortitude to withstand the onslaught or embrace the blessing. I wake up each day with more hunger from the day before. I know how lucky I am to get to open my eyes and try again. The simple fact is, we go to bed never knowing what is next. We can only do our best on this given day and hope it is enough to carry us into the next one. I'm no prophet or saint. I'm nothing more than a man with a temptation to feel everything and go after anything my soul cares for. I wish it were easier for us. I wish life didn't take out its frustration on those who already have a lifetime's worth of agony attached to their name and face. I see it all the time. I feel it even more so. I only speak to those who I feel as though can speak back to me in a way that we both walk away from the conversation knowing we are better because of it. Again, being selfish is okay. I urge you not to be reluctant when it comes to your time or spending it where you know it won't help you. Humans will speak about you either way. You might as well be doing what you love and when they do. Projection and regression of self are real things. You can walk down the street or have someone in your family who are doing it. I know you won't be reading this book until the fall, but I hope this new moon casts a beautiful light and magic upon you and the journey you find yourself on. I hope it shines forever. I hope there is a residue it leaves behind that makes you believe in the light and your own light when all else fades away and becomes nothing but a reminder of what was once here to help you through it. I hope by the time you read this, you will look back and see how far you have come with it all, with everything you once worried about becoming nothing more than a motivational tool that got you here today. You deserve it. There will be days when you do not feel as though you do, but you will always be worthy of this life, this love, this life. I am so proud of you and how far you have come and what you have overcome. Growing up, I didn't get a lot of reinforcement. Most of my good fortune was self-made. I learned at a very young age there is no one here to save you. There is no one that will ever protect you as you can. You must become the motivator for your own actions. I am sure others may be able to help and assist you in that area, but at the end of the day, it is just you and yourself. We come into this world alone and we will die the same way. It is all up to us. I enjoy the pressure it adds. I thrive in it. It is something we are not necessarily born with, but it is something we learn how to adapt to once we are thrown into the flames for the first time. Our life depends on our dependency for our own truth. We are the mind and heart of a universe trying to figure out how to survive, trying to search for a cure for all of this ache being felt in every corner of the world. We are the scientists, all hoping to find something we can love enough to hold onto forever and call it magic. There is no easy way or right way to live. Even the wealthiest of humans suffer. They all hurt and die like we will. Chin up, heart out.

Chapter VIII

-POETRY-

i probably talk too much for some and not enough for you. full moons cause me to lose my mind at times. to be consumed by that much light is to be loved in every life you almost died in before. there is you and everything else my hands cannot touch.   men like me aren't supposed to get second tries at loving the same thing twice, but i feel as though the angels i talk to know more about it than i do. you didn't save me. you gave me reasons to embrace who i didn't know how to be. you have been a healer of me.

there are days i wish to only hold you
and not say a single word. those are
the days i look forward to the most.
my life is as simple as i want it to be,
though with you, i am holding onto
the reason why my lungs continue to
battle through the madness they find
themselves in when you are not close
to me. they cry out like new born
babies who have been born from
darkness, only to have been kissed by
your light. you are the color of every
star still in love   with the absence of
hope. maybe one day they will come
to know your name as i have and
keep your magic safe, my moon.

in my head, it all worked out. all the smiles when you were near, my face has forgotten how to make love appear where you placed it. my eyes sag below the life i am living. my movements are paused, and i am lost again. keep me safely. lately i have been fading. i have been feeling you slipping away from me. catch me again, with wide eyes, with surprise gripping your heart, ready to ignite at any moment. i will do my best to keep you on my shoulders and above it all. i'll keep you from lonely, if you keep loving it out of me.

i am leaving everything behind, everyone to fend for themselves. i am letting go of anything that has pulled me down to the depths i was drowning in this year. you won't catch me in the water this coming year. i will be on firm and solid ground for the first time in years. thank you to those who left me, whom without, i would still be holding space for your ghost. thank you to those who never cared to check in on me, it allowed me a chance to see what it felt like to be completely alone and without saving. thank you to those who were too busy to help me   or even take time to reply back to me. it taught me how it feels to finally have a clean and evenly laid circle to stand in. i notice everything. it is simple, if i am not a priority in your life, you can make damn sure you will never be one in mine. my typewriters will be keeping me company moving forward. i am tired of what humanity does to each other when there is an agenda being played out.

there is only the moon left for me to give you. after all this time, her shine has lived inside of you. love is only love if we accept it ourselves before anyone else. i have been able to do that since you found me underneath a sky with no stars to be seen. love is the last thing i thought anyone could give me, until you unearthed my heart and gave it back to me. we are a universal reply given to bonded souls.

it is while watching these colors in front of me that i remember you most. this life may be a dream, but we are living in it now. we are alive with intentions on becoming something more than a face with wandering eyes and weary hearts. there are a million ways to tell someone you love them. i hope we get each one together. i hope love goes beyond the definition of what others have shown us it to be. i do not have much to give these days besides an ongoing war inside of my mind, but there is a white flag in the distance i am trying to make peace with.

some escape to leave something behind, while i personally escape to discover something new. today is a day i have waited for. the life of a wanderer is one that never ends. you search for music, art, and connection of any type. we are all searching for something. we may never know or get close to any of it, but as long as we are alive, we must try. we must give a valiant effort before the final sun appears to kiss us goodbye.

when she finds you in the morning, there is a glimpse of heavenly reverie. there is a feeling that comes over you to allow you a chance of taking it all in before the day begins. the nakedness is not to be taken for granted. as easy it comes, it leaves with such an abrupt power, you are left with nothing more than flesh removed from your soul. you are split in-half by the sheer force of its exist. you may become whole again, but you will never again see or feel her lovingly morning light.

when love becomes you, the earth remains still, yet my soul is stirred, always moving to the way your eyes look around to see nature come to life in the early attack of light. another sunrise by your side, she sits there with me, holding my hand and keeping it from shaking. we are all recovering from something. my addictions brought me hell itself, but you brought me a closeness and shaded me from its fire. my consumption of your pureness has kept the rest of the world from devouring my heart.

i go to sleep and awake in the most vivid of dreams. you, my hands sliding up then down your back, your chest, all the way to your thighs. before you're about to speak for me, i awake in a reality where my hands are useless and refuse to move for anyone except you. living in a nightmare. dreaming in a dream. i wouldn't say you haunt me, but you linger here quite often. where you go whenever you leave me with my breathing steady and heavy, it is by far the most painful part. i know already unfortunately, it's where he is and i am not.

take your heart out and relax the hurt. may your life never go back to where you feel unwanted, never seen for the the wildness you are. take your wings out from time to time to touch the sun, to undo the breaking, to believe in the fire inside of you. you have become this force, and i hope you only live and love with hurricanes. it is where your center has always been. it is where the birds and nature in me finally feel safe and secure.

i know life has become a darker shade of unknown feelings. we all need to remember how much we have already been through. you will always be enough. where you have been is a thing of the past. for it is ashes to ashes and dust to dust. i have been patient with what the world has given to me. through all of the bullshit, the truth shall set me free. i feel born again, rising up like the phoenix. a brand new day with the sun on my face, oh, what a wonderful place this is for me. stay strong and beautiful. smile through all the hardships this universe has given to you. today is your day. it doesn't belong to them anymore. dance in the fire and let it consume your soul. there is nothing more contagious than a burning spirit. after all of these years and all of the tears, use them for your garden and grow it with love. even the most darkest of days bring out the stars. even in the most darkest of places, flowers will be found, flowers will sing of glory.

there may never be another time in your life when the sunlight is as sweet as it is now. welcome in the change. become the love you'll always need and won't ever have to seek out. i don't need promises of any kind. i just need you to show up with as much love for me as you did yesterday. you are enough, a million suns, moons, and lifetimes, you are enough. you will never have to wonder what my thoughts are and where they go when you see me staring off into your golden glow.

we will never be able to love enough, to live enough, to become the truest version of our soul. but to know this day is more reason to never surrender, gives this blood of mine hope in the war. talk to me and tell me about the story that made you who you are. tell me about your bones and how they got their lovely structure. tell me how you were born with strength not to break while holding so much love above your head in hopes of someone finally seeing it and taking it from you, so you can rest in full.

as we venture out into a new year,
may we never forget our wings and
how wild it is to trust their love for
flight. i have wanted to find love in
the madness, in the chaos, in the
dreams that should have died by now.
i am a wanderer with a war machine
for a heart. i'll die in your eyes as
many times as it takes for you to
know i am never leaving your side,
for you to know you will infinitely
be kept alive in mine.

hopefully this loss of you is just passing through to the other side of truth where there's something good to remember what we had. the ocean's worth of absence i feel makes fresh air hurt more the deeper it goes down into these contused lungs, spun together by twine and rotted pine. all i can do is stare at the sun until it becomes you, until orange turns a shade of blue.

throughout life, we come across those who give our hearts a new beat, a new voice to learn and speak. time comes and goes as the sun turns another year. we become scarred and scared by our journey, by the absence only love can cure and heal. fate never makes a mistake when it comes to gathering two souls meant to be together. you are the light within my darkness, a lantern of a thousand moons giving me hope to cling to. our story is just beginning, but it's becoming something more than any poet could ever give his life to. your life is and has always been a part of me, my hands, my feet, my eyes, my movements. all of who i am does not work properly without your breathing next to me. who i am means nothing if it isn't living to get closer to you. you are the best day of my life. finding each other when we did, only leads me further into this love with you. wherever we go, a bond is set between our bones, between our promises to be here until nothing is left but the imprint of who we grew to be. love may be several things, though in the end, it's you and the comfort you give to the uncomfortable parts of me. you are the cure to the ache, to the disintegration of this body.

i know this isn't ideal. i need you to know i am here. i'll tell you all i can so you know when you think i am not thinking about you, it is all i am consumed with. i am not here to write you pretty words for the rest of my life and that be all we become. i want a life with you, even if it is merely a pipe dream for me now. i want to take advantage of our presently time, and whenever we have it. i cannot promise you more than that, but i will get on one knee and ask you for your soul to marry mine. seeing your morning energy and feeling your rapture this early during the day, whatever you want, it is the same thing as me.

i hear there's a gunfight outside by the bar. a coal miner and a logger got into it over a hand of poker. everyone's waiting on the trigger to be pulled and see who is face down when the smoke clears. sirens wail out, blue and red in the parking lot. victory was laid to rest when pride got in the way of letting it go.   the coal miner had a full house. the logger had four of a kind, but he slipped an extra king into the game when everyone was occupied getting drinks. now both are face down, bleeding out, crying for second chances and their dead mothers to save them. the pot got up to fifty thousand before guns were drawn. the waitress smiles at them both, gives them a side eye and a wink. fifty thousand reasons to never come back to work. she's gone.

i wish you could love me. not me begging on my knees and hands folded in as if you are god almighty himself and i am the other child he had out of wedlock, asking for some goddamn attention. i wish you could love me like you do him, like you once used to when loving me was all you knew. why is   it so hard to look me in the eyes when mine search for you before light moves the darkness aside. the landscape and foliage inside of me is dying of drought, of forgotten ways you once told me about when it came to nursing the war i was covered with. i wish you could love me again, in the same arms you are using to hold him. if this is what dying feels like, i wish you'd just leave me here to take you in one last time. heaven sent or hell-bent, it all ends the same way when love is in the middle of it.

you will never know what you need until it's gone, until it no longer is there for you as you said it would be. love is a lot of things, but one thing it isn't, is attempting to sabotage someone into believing they are crazy for thinking for their own sake. she is a wild card, a heart on on both sleeves. she will continue flying amongst the birds and angels, because that's where she belongs. it is a home no one else will ever destroy. it is peace, safety, comfort, all in the shape of freedom. give her sunsets and sunrises. give her anything she can remember and look back on to know it all works out and is worth it. to know moving forward, flowers will still grow in the winter's bloom when you have to go out to gather wood and beauty for the inside of your home to keep everything else alive. there will be days when you won't know if she is all wolf, all unicorn, or all moon. when you are unsure of it, trust in the fact she can be all three at any given time. she is love in every form, in god's whispers, in the universe's third eye, in the ocean's infinity blue.

i don't know how to live without you, to love if it isn't you. i wander these streets at night, hoping to catch your reflection in the light before it steps back into the truth i already know it to be. i am a master of nothing, but mastering a life full of your absence is one thing i will need to perfect if i am ever going to hold a new warmth, a new body, a new life when meeting you didn't completely fucking destroy me.

these words have always been for you
and about you. if it weren't for you,
these pages would still be as naked
and empty as i was the day you found
me. i know i would go mad, fucking
insane to the bone without you.
you are the woman i have named
books after, the reason i know the
moon as well as i do, and placed
flowers in a vase for the sun to love as
much as i do. take these cold nights
from my life. i have exhausted all of
my options and now i am left with
nothing but a scavenger's mindset.
i will remain on this path until
i find the heart of it all, until i find
the heart of you to love evermore.

i used to think being alone would be my life   forever. i took it as a fucking punch to the soul. knowing how much i crave closeness, it took more out of me to understand not all of us will come to know it as a friend, as a lover. the more i meet other humans, i learn i have saved myself countless years of frustration and angst. self-preservation is an acquired taste, as is giving your heart away. it is such a rebellious act these days. the mere thought of it splits the earth in two, giving one side of the darkness to me and one to you. it has become an unparalleled balance not to question, but to learn from, to walk with as i go on without light to guide me. you were once my home, now i am orphaned all over again. a single sunset that gives me comfort and shelter, is all i am after these days.

become the lion and go about your life. it is too short to be around those who feed off of you, instead of helping you feed yourself. time moves on without your permission, without your signature of approval. i wish there was a way to give back to a life that has given me more than i know what to do with at times. be easy on yourself. not all can be done in a lifetime. not everything is meant to happen now. be present with the time and space you are in. it is still a living and breathing miracle to witness such bliss, such tragedy, such unknowns.

i'm not sure if this is love or merely a passing of souls. you make me forget all of the pain and discomfort i deal with on a daily basis. your presence alone teaches my lonely how to cope with everything i am and everything i am not. i can be stuck in my head for days if i am not careful with my intentions, but you make it better by being open with me about your struggles. i am just a man looking for a place to rest his head and worries when all i know for certain is death becomes another make-believe tale as your body gives me a proper peace. you are the walls and windows to a home i never had at any given moment in my entire life. the closest thing i had was an idea of what one was like from the times i spent the night at my best friend's house. even then i wasn't sure, but i know now what it was supposed to hold on the inside and look like on the outside.

it's a rare and delicate occurrence,
finding someone like you with such
a gift for living as freely as you do. i've
learned a lot in our brief time
together. you have shown me how to
believe in my human, the entirety
of my awkward showing of my
humanness. you have shown me
how my darkness and light can dance
and coexist together, regardless of my
inability to care for both at times.
i now know life is temporary and love
is forever when you find someone
who does all they can to extend
your longevity, because they know
how many times you've died before
you got here where everything is
lovely and unhurried.

i'm going to love you well beyond the means of who i am. long after the trees surrender themselves for winter. long after the bees forget who they are and where their flowers migrated to. long after the wind becomes nothing more than a washed away hurricane during a dormant season of the dead living harmlessly and walking amongst its captives. i want it to be you when i ask, "for the rest of our lives?"

i spoke with you earlier and told you how proud i am of you and for you. not many who chose the path you did, would have been able to make it as far as you have. many would've folded up or unfolded the white flag kept neatly between a ribcage made from broken kingdoms. but not you. it's never your style. you have always left it all in the ring. i will accompany you for however long you need a friend in me. now i understand certain kinds of love are better to be carried inside of a heart rather than in the hand or on a finger. i am proud of you, sweet may. there was a time you were the moon, but now you are a sky full of stars. i will continue holding space for you. there is nothing i wouldn't do to make sure your eyes never knew another tear or your heart knew another ache to grasp.

this season continues on without new feelings to embrace. i feel as though i have been stuck in time, three years behind anyone seeking refuge or looking to find closure from an unknown endangerment. i am all human more times than not. i am all soul when the day calls for me to become something greater for those in my life and for myself. the sky is crooked today with humidity soaking the trees of a promise they carry for all of us to find one day. today is Saturday, partly cloudy, full of dead grass and wildlife rummaging the side of the roads looking for food of any kind. i love Texas, but every state has an expiration date when it becomes unbearable for you, while stunting any type of mental growth and stimulation. the weather this year has been overwhelming, suffocating bones of the living and the dead in soil hardening by the day. a few cracks here and there. you'd think a sinkhole would appear to take you away for good. the one thing nothing can take away is this remembrance i have for you and of you. it was around this time eight years ago we first found each other. it was around seven years ago i first drove out there to see you. it was around five years the last time i flew out to see you. it was around four years ago now since i last saw you. we were in the booth and i knew then what i still know when we first met, it's you. you are my happy everything even if we cannot be together. i will go down in ash and flame knowing a truth, but only getting a few moments of it becoming our bodies on each other. if missing someone this much can redirect your path, i can only imagine if things would have worked out and you fought for me, instead of him.

i want my words to feel like rustling of leaves in the last pile of fall you made then jumped into, because there was nothing left to do bu to feel your youth again. other times, i want them to feel like an inferno you are in the middle of, knowing what you are feeling is everything you have forgotten about. i want you to feel it all before burying it somewhere no one else will find, not even you. i need you to let go of the past you tied up and made sit in the corner for it to reflect on itself. you deserve to know how beginning again feels like when it comes from someone who has watched your whole life amass from regrets. you are greater than the bond between our sun and moon. who you are is a reverie to me.

there was a moment you knew the fighting was over, the day was won. you had victory in your hands and the sun bleeding red. there was an unspoken beating you never mentioned before, but your eyes held it tightly as i watched you fight it nightly. your bruises soaked through your love and it got to the point you nearly gave up on yourself, on everyone. i know what being broken feels like. i know what it looks like. i know how it stays with you regardless of the good in you, despite the good in you. you've turned dusk to dawn, changing how the birds sing their songs. you are the church for every sin and wrong i've done. you are the first sight of love after everyone else has gone.

Chapter IX

M.T.W.T.F.S-

Today is Tuesday. Another week has came and gone. My mental health is still riding stable and my mind is at ease with what and who is in my world. I know bad times do not last forever, just as the good times must end. The way life is set up, is a directionless compass we tend to move the needle ourselves in order to make right of the choices we make and will make. I could write all day and beyond the very next, with every thought prior to this one being meaningless since I have already changed from the day before. I have always thought about how we are all connected and intertwined together. Each individual living their own distinct life and no life ever repeated. We walk these streets and sidewalks seeing everyone at least once and never seeing them again. Somehow we believe it was meant to be. Somehow we know the importance this individual will play in our lives. Be it a glance, a few more seconds than that, or a lingering stare as you almost break your neck to keep them in your view for as long as you can. Every kind of beauty does   that to us. Inside and out. It rearranges us as we knew ourselves previously. It is such a beautiful, intimate moment with who we are at that moment. We forget anything else going on in our lives, because our attention gravitates towards a connection we know nothing about. The familiarity between locking eyes with a stranger across the way is all it takes for us to know we are where we are needed. That somehow, this exact moment being alive was a choice already made years ago when it all could've ended abruptly. The breakfast we ate, how long it took for us to eat. The time it took to shower and pick out a pair of jeans, shirt, shoes, and whatever else we thought we needed. Our concise decisions, however big or small at the time, lead us to these moments of inclusion, of feeling as though we do fucking belong here. That our story is not over yet, all based off an emotional impulse to not give your eyes back to yourself just yet. To belong to something other than yourself for a brief breath, then you are back on your way, thinking how incredible it was to see someone and they see you, too. I believe in fate, in meant to be. Coincidences do not happen because of happenstance or lack of meaning. There are no such things in my beliefs. Maybe these occurrences have happened before in some other lifetime, in another world before we were in this one. My deep thoughts only fall deeper into whatever abyss I am consumed with at the time. To believe in anything, there must be a reason for it behind the reason we give. Possibly we were taught these things we carry around like a schoolbag full of loose leaf paper and folders without subjects on them. I was born with thoughts and images already inside of me. It took me a while to figure out what deja vu actually meant to me. It wasn't only something happening for the second time. It was something happening for the first time in this world, but being overwhelmed by your soul experiencing it in this reality. The thoughts continue to go deeper into the chasm, but at times, I know I need to reign them in or else I will be diving into a space of earth I may never return from. I'm trying to remain balanced most days with a clear mind and clean soul. All the hurt and darkness I am made out of tends to rock me back to the edge of the mind where love is nonexistent and hope hangs by a noose covered in a remembrance of what it all used to mean to me. There are no easy stages in life. Each one we go through asks something more of us as we get older. I have only known of hard times and hand-me-down opinions made by those too fucking scared or ignorant to have their own. My shyness is upfront. I do not pretend to be an outgoing human. I'd much rather spend my time sitting here in this chair, typing away. It has never been about safety for me in the sense of not wanting to be around others. My choices have made me this way. I have trusted too easily and too much. I opened up my walls for those who should've remained on the outside for a lifetime and never been allowed in. They stole my joy, my happiness, along with every single lantern I had hanging up to not lose my way inside. Being born in the dark is one thing. It is entirely different once you have been aware of the light and know what it is capable of, then going without it for a stretch of your life. It tends to happen to me every ten years or so. I am going on year five of this episode. It has been the most tortuous one. When you love someone and they love you, you think it will be okay. You think you can tell them everything you have never told anyone else before and it will be safe and held with a adoration that can sustain it. You think once you open up the gates, the only thing coming in or going out are the carriages bringing in copious amounts of energy and beauty to match what you're giving away basically for free. Thieves are not all the same. Some steal whatever they can for the sake of their own survival. Others know what they're after and will take by any means necessary, even if it means annihilating everything and everyone in its path. I am rebuilding from the ground up. My feet were not made for walking before I found her. But now I am fucking running wherever I go. I am about to make a late lunch, then settle in for the evening. At the end of my day, I know I have exhausted every ounce of who I am by giving this medium its rightly due. The weather seems to be getting warmer and the humidity is laughing at us all. The electric bill came in today. The house I live in has no insulation. The windows are not pressed plumb against their mounts. Hot air gets in here fairly easily. For some reason, the owners of this house previously made a fireplace but forgot to add a damper, which closes off the outside air and dirt and whatever else from getting inside. It is a janky house, but one that houses what we need and keeps what we need safe. Our bill was less than one hundred dollars, which if you knew how long the air condition stayed on, you would think it was some type of joke, but it was a huge relief. This summer has been the hottest one on record for where I live. We were able to turn the air down to seventy-six last night. We typically leave the house on eighty-three during the day, then lower it to seventy-eight before bed. It is nice to splurge on something like that. It must be cold in my room to feel rested, but when you grow up and are born suffering, you learn to live with things less than most can or want to. I told my dad last night that once you know how to suffer in life, you learn something most never will. It isn't a bad thing to me. I think a lot of us become too comfortable and not enough know what being uncomfortable actually is. All of these millionaires and billionaires, yet there are so many homeless and dying because they cannot buy food. I read something today about the amount of money Lewis Hamilton has spent. He is a famous Indy car driver. Three homes, eight sports cars, a few being highly priced due to them being limited editions. A few speed boats and several other things. I cannot imagine having that much wealth. Maybe that is why I do not have it. I would do too much good with it and spend less on materialistic things that wouldn't make me happy anyway. If I had the means, I would open a veteran's shelter and other homeless shelters around the country. I would do anything I could to make sure someone was getting the same chances as I was to succeed. Not everyone will be able to help, I know. But it seems unjust so many are going without, especially now, and several others are spoiling themselves to no end. I am not condemning them. I don't judge anyone. I am simply saying if I had the money of some rich human, I would make sure to give back. I am sure they give to charities and what not, but I would want to be on the front lines making sure these humans, our own kind, were being taken care and not thrown away to make room for someone else who has it better. I used to believe we were all equal. Obviously that isn't the case and never was. Going back to ancient times and predating the first human, nothing was equal. Someone or something was always trying to gain an edge or upper-hand to ensure themselves of making it out alive and living longer than the rest of those who were trying to survive. We must look out for another if we are to make this world tolerable for the next to follow. Especially in today's climate, with the pandemic, new wars, new things to get pissed of about daily like the national debt and every crisis under the sun. I can only hope the newbies who grow up find a way to live and actually know what happiness feels like. The last year especially has felt like doom, with negative energy at every corner. I hope they make it out okay. Not everyone will be able to sustain themselves. Regardless of the amount of time and energy they place into their lives and no matter how much they prioritize their needs. The good in you will be found and sought after by any kind looking for refuge. Be careful of those who you let in. Some come to us and look for forgiveness for what they have done by being able to have someone love them the way they have always needed. Others come to us seeking to destroy what they can, because it is who they have been their entire lives. There is no middle ground for these seekers. Be cautious, but open to your own feelings and emotions in the same breath. It feels as though I have lived a thousand lives in one and everything I ever loved has came and went. Lonely is a fucking miserable place to find yourself in. But at the same time, there is another kind of place you can find yourself in. It is found in-between wanting to be with someone and not wanting to share your space with anyone else. It is one of the strangest dynamics a human can live with. You know you want love and whatever else tags along with it. Your heart may second guess it before your mind does. You may be open to it all, but once you speak of love for the first time with them, you cringe. Not out of spite or terror, but out of being afraid you are giving up too much of your freedom by giving someone else a piece of it. I cannot tell you how to give away your heart and soul. I will never tell anyone what they should do with them. I have been asked a million times myself that question. I respond to it in the same manner as the first time someone asked me for advice. I tell them, all we can do is live for ourselves and hope we find someone who wants to be a part of it without changing who we are, without changing the course and path we are on. We want to believe everyone we meet will meet us where we are at and not drag us further into a place we just got out of. We want fresh, something to breathe in that our lungs will accept. I do not live by life quotes or self-help books. I never understood them. I know they are popular and probably the book of choice for many of us. It always seemed odd to me that you are reading something from someone else who may or may have not lived a life worthy of traveling, yet you eat up their words because you know you won't ever be brave enough to try it on your own. I do not believe in living someone else's life or experiences. It is a counter-intuitive approach to why we are here in my opinion. We are here to live and create our own story, our own character, our own memories. I guess some of us choose safety over the unknown. I do   not care what you do. I simply hope you choose something for yourself and not something that is influenced by others. It is the death before the actual one comes to tell you it's time. I personally want to be able to tell someone I lived my life my way. Not doused in someone else's choices and words. It is one of the main reasons I do not read as much as some to do these days. I cannot tell you the last time I actually bought a book or read one that gave me hope. My favorite writers are all dead. Hemingway, Neruda, Cohen, Kerouac, Ginsberg, the beat writers, the truth seekers, the adventurists who doubled down on their own path and convictions. That is where the soul is found. It is where we come to know who we are. When it is just you and the reflection staring back at you, do you know who you are? Do you live your life as someone else has told you to? I'd like to think my choices were all a matter of fact and instantaneous. Something in the gut tells you when and where to go. A veil lifts from your heart and it sings and cheers you on, because you both know what is going to happen will be the decision that changes it all for you. The sightly dance with fate and its own soul. We may never get to where we are going, but I do know if you rely on someone else to get there, you will be drifting in an abyss with depths that will drown you. Your skill will only take you so far. The life you live will get you the rest of the way. This book I am writing, the one you will be reading this fall, is a combination of doing something I have wanted to do since I was a kid and putting it off until I felt the time was ready to share these parts of myself openly. These are all thoughts I have had or am having in the present moment. It is the rawest form of the written word to me. To know yourself means having scars to prove you were alive once. The stories they keep for you are not for everyone to read, and if they do end up reading them, they will never understand regardless of how much you pretty up what you've been through. I only know how to write one way. Though I have written in other forms for someone I once loved. There is a difference and others can see it, feel it, and will call you out on it. It is why I laugh and smirk at these humans who aren't even thirty yet, who haven't even had a real scar to show and tell. They don't know what hell is. They don't know what going down the highway at a speed around ninety can make you feel. They sit back with words from afar, but they sell it to you. More power to them for making something believable. All I know is reality changes for us once we open our eyes to it. We may never know anything close to the love we grew up with. For some, I am sure they never want to experience anything resembling it for the lack of it being there to begin with. My personal tale of love is knowing and never knowing it all. One day it was warm arms wrapped tightly around me, keeping my dreams and fear of life itself from getting too far out of control. The next day it was someone waking up sober and apologizing for the night prior and telling me it would never happen again. I went my entire life living on eggshells, broken, scattered, and misplaced throughout the floors of our home. It was a panic room full of anxiety and misconception. My older brother is three years older than I am. There were days when we wouldn't talk at all. I look back at my younger days and who we were, and I am amazed we have the bond we do now. We were distant growing up. I don't actually recall any type of brotherly love between us unless it was playing video games past midnight or heading to a basketball or football game we were playing in. As we got older, it only got worse. My mother got worse as well. She took a lot of her frustration out on us because there was nowhere else she could place it once the alcohol was done for the day. When my brother was seventeen, my mom kicked him out of the house for having a woman over and they shut the door to his room. I was in the living room and all I heard was yelling and cussing and the smell of natural light beer, along with whatever lotion the girl he had over was wearing. Eventually, he walked outside and got into his truck, then left. My mom was yelling and hitting his window, telling him to get out and fuck this and fuck that. It is one of the most profound images I have in my head that plays like some home video you leave in the attic, but the heat and rats cannot destroy. Every once and a while, I will think about that moment during my childhood and still know it was a changing of the guard in a lot of ways. He never returned. He never came back to check on my younger brother and I. He ended up living with a friend the rest of the year and his entire senior year. The only time I would see him would be at school, and even then, he didn't want anything to do with me. I was friends with some of his friends so he had to put up with me most of the time. I took it personally as did my younger brother. It was just him and I to defend and counter whatever my mother was doing to us. She eventually started to give my younger brother most of the grief and mind games. I did all I could to keep him safe, as well as make sure I was okay and safe from it all. I remember looking through the blinds on the door and seeing her out there smoking her cigarettes and drinking her beer. They were the kind of blinds on the door that made it difficult for me to keep an eye on her to make sure I could give my brother a heads up in case she was on one of her episodes. But it never escalated beyond the mental and verbal abuse. As we got older, bigger, stronger, and less afraid of her antics, we were able to control it. It took a few years, but we got there. He and I suffered together for years, which is why our bond is stronger than anything else in this world. He is my best friend and that won't ever change. Unfortunately, my older brother and I never could sustain a brotherly relationship growing up and beyond our teenage years. Once he moved out, we hardly spoke and I don't recall him ever checking on us. To have someone you love leave you like that, who is blood and family, it leaves the worst break in your heart. Looking back and even then, I understood why he did what he did. It wasn't until I graduated high-school did I realize it. When I was sixteen, my brother and I got kicked out of the house the first time for doing nothing. My mother felt as if she needed to do it for whatever reason. She was really struggling the years after my parent's divorce. I was eleven, turning twelve when it happened. I remember calling my father and hiding underneath a desk in my older brother's old room to make the call. It was the most uneasy I have ever felt in my life. I didn't know what she was capable of truthfully, especially when she began drinking more and more. He flew in to Dallas and drove down to pick us up the next night. We walked down the hallway, past my mother's room, and I glanced inside it. I saw her in her bed, sheets pulled up to her neck, eyes as red as the devil's if it had any to reflect hell. She didn't say a single word. We left and the next seven months, we stayed with my dad and his fiance at the time in St. Croix, USVI. life was simpler there. It was calmer. It was everything a teenager probably never gets to experience in any given lifetime. They tried to give us a life we never had and maybe one my dad was trying to make up for, since he was barely around during any of it. I felt the guilt he had lived with for all of those years. I know he was doing all he could to make sure we felt safe and were loved. Which I knew he did love us. Having his job, it was nearly impossible to do anything but travel in order to get the work done and make enough money to sustain the household. We enrolled into the school there. We began making friends a few weeks after getting a chance to settle in. Being an athlete along with my younger brother, it made it easier to fit in a lot of ways. Basketball season was just beginning. The day we left our mother's house, it was also basketball season. Once the season started there, it was an easy transition. It wasn't the biggest school, so if you could play sports, it was a big deal. They had a really good team before we showed up, but my brother and I were really good as well. It was such a blast playing ball down there. Traveling around the islands, playing tournaments, living a life I never dreamt about before. It wasn't luxurious, but to us it was. After the season ended, I had already found a girlfriend and doing my best to fit in, while maintaining relationships both there and back home. There was still Yahoo Messenger during that time. I got on there a few times a day to check on my friends I had known my entire life to make sure they were okay. Things didn't end up working out there unfortunately. My younger brother wanted to go back, which meant I had to as well. I was never going to allow him to go back without me, so it was a given agreement. My mother told us she had changed and was doing better than ever before. Both he and I were missing our friends, but I wanted to stay. I never told him that because I didn't want him to feel guilty or feel as though he was hurting me in any way. It was one of the toughest decisions I ever had to make. But taking care of him and making sure my mother didn't fuck with him was my main priority. Your family is all you have. When there is a fracture in the system, it can either ruin it all or bring you closer together. I'm a huge advocate for everything happening for a reason. I allow it to be the leading light in my life. It served me then just as it does to this day. When we got back, my mom, her best friend and her kids, which we were friends with, picked us up. It all seemed like smooth sailing from there. Being home the first night, I was actually terrified of being there and knew I didn't want to be anywhere near that place. It took a few months for things to go back to the way it was. My hair was long and bleached out due to the sun and ocean life from the islands. My ears were pierced as well, as was my brother's ears. Our school didn't allow it so we had to take them out once classes began. The first sign of normalcy was met with my mom showing her true colors at the moment. It all came crashing down and I was forced to ask my best friend if I could move in with him. My brother was forced to ask a teacher if he could move in with him.

My entire senior year and my brother's next two years would be spent away from our mother. There was almost a restraining order given to her, but luckily the incident went without needing one. The entire year is a blur to me to be honest. I was drinking a lot more, taking pills, and smoking weed regularly. My junior year of high school is one I wish I could redo again. I chose the party life instead of focusing on playing sports and myself. I didn't even play football that year. I woke up hungover the day of two-of-days and made the choice not to play. Everyone was pretty shocked by it. I had lost a lot of weight being in the islands. I probably weighed in around 160lbs or 165lbs if I had to guess. That is after being around 200lbs and 215lbs during that time of year before with all the weightlifting and sport activities I was doing. I survived daily.

Everyone knew about what was going on in my life because being in a small town, people take it upon themselves to know every single fucking detail to gossip about. At the end of the year, I promised myself to refocus my life and get back to playing football and doing better in school. Which I was a Honor Roll kid. I just slacked off a bit and ruined my chances of getting any kind of scholarship at the end of my senior year because I didn't apply myself as I should have. My senior year came and went faster than any year of my life. I was still partying and hanging out with my friends, but in a more manageable way. My balance was better. I had a girlfriend before all of this happened and it was strenuous work to say the least. Living with my best friend and partying as much as I had been, her and I barely saw each other, but eventually I ended up choosing more time with her. It didn't last long because of timing. When I was kicked out for the second time, I knew her and I wouldn't make it, but I wanted to try because she deserved it. She was a Christian girl as were her parents. Super religious and strict. She was one of the smartest humans in school, which meant her studies would come first because that was what her father wanted. I never wanted to bring her down in any way. I knew her plan was college and becoming a lawyer of some kind. The end of the year came and we tried to make it work. She ended up going to school at LSU and I went to Blinn Community College in College Station, Texas with my best friends. Which was another disaster. I am laughing while typing this since a lot of memories are flooding me today. It was some of the best and worst times of my life. Mostly the good ones shine through nowadays. I will leave that part there and begin writing somewhere else tomorrow. Reflection is the greatest form of self-awareness. Without it, we are drifting further away from who we are. We must maintain a balance at all costs. It only costs you your time, but if you want to survive the hell you may find yourself in, you will adjust your beliefs to include what is good for you and who is good for your life. This life isn't made to be easy. It's all chaos. When the day becomes a moment you never want to let go of, you realize how deeply every feeling is and how it turns us and molds us into the human and journey we are living. It is a splendid display of power and trust we are not even aware of until the day after. We wake up feeling lighter, reinvigorated with a purpose. We walk a bit slower to catch all the signs we had missed before. We talk less and listen to every sound under the sun. We incorporate more of ourselves because we are able to see a clearer path than the wooded one we were in. Life is nothing more than lessons giving way to new uses of our skills to survive. I know each day will have a tolerance for the amount of good, just as we do. We think we want it to be smooth sailing all the time, but we know if it is, we won't ever develop as humans. There needs to be tragedy. There needs to be trauma. There needs to be sadness eloping with a sour mood. I don't know anyone who has nothing but good days there entire lives. If I would have came across someone like that, it would have been a quick exchange of pleasantries, then leaving not ever knowing any differently. I am attracted to beauty, yes, but I need to see suffering inside eyes that may have lived something similar as I had been accustomed to being around. The connection needs to be made then and there. The same goes for sex with me. If there isn't a connection, nothing will ever come of it. There is nothing to gain for me by giving my body and soul away to someone who doesn't know what they are doing. If they do, they aren't there for anything else but the act itself. Today is more like it has been the previous weeks, more sun, more humidity, more of what we don't need at the moment. I cannot tell you the last time it rained. I cannot tell you the last time I went anywhere besides the post office and grocery store. Being alive is one thing, but being alive and aware of what you are doing is sufficient enough to sustain forward momentum is another. Routines are deadly. Probably the most deadly thing we can do to ourselves if we are unable to get out of our own way for a while. I am dying for a getaway. I need some personal time alone with myself. It has been too long since I looked myself in the mirror and asked how I was doing. Caring about everyone and not yourself is also a death sentence. I've served a few in my lifetime already and it is something you think you can break and become your own way once and for all. It hasn't been easy being the giver, the helper, the one everyone turns to when shit hits the fan and they are covered in their own bullshit. I remain this way for myself. I know it is my best version, especially the sober kind. The wind is a quiet hush today. It is still spilling clouds all over the sky as it tips them over one by one. The blue is a bit more turquoise, a hint of a healed bruise, with room to improve in a lighter shade if it wanted to. I honestly do not know where these pages are going before I begin one. I don't intentionally plan on skipping around, but I enjoy breaking up the stories with other real life aspects to give credence to my mood and see where my mind is at during these sessions. Each time I write in here, it typically takes me about an hour to do so. I don't say when and where I start and begin. There is a joy I get from throwing up my guts onto paper like this. It also enacts a suffering I am familiar with. One where the memories aren't always of the bad kind, but they still hurt and cause reflection nonetheless. I imagine myself capable and finally healing one day. Being trauma free, drama free, and whatever else from my past that may find me, is something I have only known of for short periods of my life. I want to believe we all heal. I want to believe there is a full circle we come across while on our journey which deflects anything we are keeping out from ever getting back in. Maybe there is a point in this life when it all makes sense. Maybe we go through it all and never get to it in the end. I am trying not to allow it to impact me either way, but when you are still searching for answers and love, it all becomes its own entity entirely. I thought I would be with someone by now. I thought I would be waking up to my lover and we would roll around in bed for a while before getting up to see what the day had for us. Once my engagement fell through in 2010 after two years, I knew kids were not going to be in my life. It wasn't me being incapable of raising kids. It was me knowing my life would never be able to sustain that lifestyle. I made a choice then and there. Ever since then, it has been the first thing I have told to anyone I had found to be in my life. Some of them took it okay. Others wanted them. Believing in yourself and your path, you cannot allow anyone to detour you from it. Of course they can add to it, but if they know who you are and what you want, and still try to change you, they aren't for you. Love can be cyclical as well as for the cynical. I do not have any answers for those looking for something perfect out of both. We do what we can and make the best out of wherever we find ourselves at the end of the day. Being at the age I am now, there won't be anything I truly sacrifice for a greater finding of love. I have given my entire fucking life writing about it, having it, losing it, and it completely fucking destroying my life. If it isn't good for the heart and soul, leave it be, and thank it. Find a way to move on with your life still breathing and beating down the stars to get you where you need to be. I cannot tell you how much damage you can inflict upon yourself if you wait around hoping things will subside and life will get better with them being in it. I can only tell you how much of you will be left if you think sticking around for the greater good will change it. We as individuals live a life of our own forever. Even if we are with someone, at the center of it, is someone you know better than anyone else will ever get a chance to. Living on parallels of someone else is a beautiful thing. It has only happened to me once before it gave way to the bottom of an undefined ocean I barely got out of alive. I'm great at giving advice, but the worst at taking it. I just don't believe in it most days. The self-help bullshit and modern day Buddha's who haven't even died yet, they are the ones a lot of humans listen to. I know

I have spoken about it earlier in this book, but I cannot harp on it enough to make your life your own. I understand we are all struggling and trying to find a connector of sorts to tie it all in and make us feel better and less alone. I never saw where being told what to do actually helped. Whatever it is you are looking for, I do hope you find it. I know what we all seek is out there. All it takes is the best version of who you are to make it a reality. All it takes is never giving up on the dream itself to make do and settle with something you had daydreamed about the night prior that seemed like an easier thing to do. The great thing about this life, is no one really knows what the fuck they are doing. The sooner you realize it, the better off you will be at everything you think you are horrible at or don't grasp completely. Most days I want to give up and leave everything behind and relocate into the mountains to never be heard from again. The last several years have took a mental toll on me I don't often speak of, because I try and power through it. Deep down I know it isn't healthy for me to keep burying my grief and agony, hoping something beautiful and hopeful comes from it. I go through it daily. The constant feeling of spinning my wheels, wasting my time where I am, knowing I could be off somewhere else giving a better effort than I do here. One day it will come when I am maxed out with it and pack up what I can and give away what I don't want. One day it will come when you won't hear from me again. I think I would be happier if it came sooner rather than later. Society wasn't made for someone like me. All of the mental games, all of the constant outdoing of others to make yourself feel important in some sad and sadistic way. There isn't enough money in this world to save us all, and even if there were, we would still be trying to kill one another for it. As much as I love what social media has done for me, it is nothing more than poison for our souls. Checking to see if someone is living a better life than you. Checking to see what kind of news you can send to someone else to guilt trip them into believing what they are doing is wrong and horrible for the world. The constant comparing of bodies, minds, and lives. It is such a waste of my fucking time. I do my best to take my breaks, but unfortunately, I cannot stay gone for long because this space is my business and creating content is my job. I've gotten better with it this year. Posting less and writing more. I feel as though I have hit a wall with it. It is a helpless feeling knowing the reach you once had is now nothing more than a third of what you used to attain. No one sees what you do. No one honestly cares about it in the end. They can say otherwise, but I know it wouldn't matter if I stopped, because someone else would come along and take my place. That's the way it has always been for artists. Some of them will support you through thick and thin, but you know deep down, nothing would change. The world itself has changed. The pandemic changed us. I am unsure if for the good or not. Each day seems to be a seesaw effect. As soon as you feel as though it is over, it tilts back to a place you are afraid of, seeing yourself running from it because you know it isn't the place you were once familiar with. This entire year has been one step forward, then nothing to show for it except my physical endurance being more tangible. Mentally, I am exhausted. I can feel my body drained and let out into the water to aimlessly float amongst waves and whatever else can stay afloat long enough until the sun goes down. There is a fatigue I am not used to having. I can still write and be okay with it. I guess that's all that matters to me, even if no one reads it or not as many as once did before. Frustration has caused me to lose interest in posting more than I do, knowing it will only reach a few hundred people instead of the thousands it once did when social media wasn't about paying for likes and followers. It is such a scheme and trap to get lost in. I hope others do not get consumed with trying to pay for notoriety. Fame is nothing more than selling a soul to those who are cheaply bought by mediocre abilities. Some are worthy of it. Others are finding loopholes.

I'm not jealous of them. I don't envy any part of being famous. I am all about the words and feelings, trying to help someone not feel as alone as they think they are. Some artists will always put their art first before the money. I have always been told how money cannot buy you happiness. I learned a long time ago how much that statement is utter bullshit. It may not solve all your problems. It may invite more of them into your life, but I know for certain it can lessen the worry and struggle a large majority of us are dealing with on a daily basis. My happiness has never been dependent on it. I have struggled my entire life with or without it in a lot of ways. Nature is my church. It is the one place where nothing or no one judges you. Traveling has been my escape since I was little. Be it on my own or with my family moving states. There was something incredible distinct about seeing new life, new energy, new colors, new animals, new everything. It always amazed me when someone asked where I was from and why I was living where they did, as if being there was some type of indictment on me. I took it as them not fully understanding the magic that lived there amongst their eyes. Maybe they grew tired of it. I can understand that principle, because I have lived next to the ocean for years now and haven't touched sand in years. It isn't out of boredom though. It isn't because I don't respect the magnitude, the sheer openness and magnificence of it. It is simply not for me anymore. This stage, I have outgrown. I can feel it daily. The reminders are everywhere. I even have days where I resent being here and take it out on myself. I have to remind myself that it is just another season of searching. Another season of making due with what you have and being thankful for the family you still have, the breath you still breathe in, and the love of a universe for not taking you yet. The dynamic is tricky and whimsical. The reality of it all is sometimes overpowering. I have spoke about balance in this book already, but I cannot state it enough, when it comes to it being the most crucial part of a life. If it were not for my writing, I honestly do not know where I would be or what I would be doing. I have skills, and with those skills, I have limitations. I do not have a college education or anything worthy of being called higher education except for the lessons I have learned along the way. Even though those are overrated to some degree. I have people skills and communication has been something

I've worked on my entire life. Be it the silent kind where your hands show someone else   the world you've been holding and taking care of. Other times it is through eye contact when you feel someone and know whatever you are going through, they will understand because they do not shy or look away from you when you get to the tears falling down your fucking face. The cruelty some of us have lived with can only be hidden for so long until you break down in front of someone you don't even know but feel comfortable with. In a larger sense of living, I am in need of more than just someone saying they love me. I am in need of more than someone to pass the time with. I do not necessarily need adventure. A single open road will do the trick just fine. Today is the second to last stage of the Tour De France. It is something my dad and I have watched for over a decade together. It is my favorite sport to take in because of the suffering the athletes put their bodies and minds through. Over or close to one hundred miles a day on a bike for three weeks. Riding over mountains and through valleys, it is what I relate to the most. It is reaching your threshold, blowing out your guts, and going beyond it for sacrifice and victory. There isn't another sport like it. It's giving your all for glory, for a momentary realization that for one day out of the year or out of your life, you were better than 196 riders. Triumph looks different to everyone. It may feel different to someone who has experienced it on a different level. Breaking yourself entirely for a chance at immortality is golden, is admirable for the greater good of your morality. Anything less and you're dead already. This is the last week of July. I cannot get over how quickly these months are passing us. With everything going on in the world at the moment, you sometimes forget about your own little world within it. You forget to tend to yourself and make sure you are complete and whole. Every day is another chance, another opportunity to seize control of your desires. Each day is another blessing even though I am not a religious man, I do trust in a universe that never hands out mistakes or gives you misinformation if you pay attention closely. It is all valuable assets for our journey, for this crowded adventure of discovery. I have been focusing more and more on my mental and physical health. The mental part of it comes with my writing and making sure I am dedicating my time to create more content. Not to necessarily share, but to look back on to see growth at any level I can be proud of. The physical prospect of it comes in the morning when I dedicate at least two to two and a half hours to priming my body to remain in the best shape as possible. I once worked out twice or three times a day before age became something my body couldn't run away from. I may be only thirty-six, and by the time this book comes out, I will be thirty-seven, my body has been through decades of war with self and life. My back gives me issues. My hips follow suit, as well as my left foot. I cannot begin to even estimate how many miles I have accumulated over the years. I cannot even begin to fathom the amount of hours I have put into these bones and on this heart and mind. I know if I don't work my mind and body, I am useless and fatigue sets in on the heaviest levels imaginable. This is my entire life. I don't have a support team other than my family, and even that is more than most these days. I do not have a team to help me with social media or shipping or anything to do with my work. It all falls on me. The success and failure of what I do depends on my aptitude to sustain it all. Being a creator is one thing. Being a writer is another entirely different beast. Anyone can write, sure, but if you are writing for the sake of doing it, you are misusing it and abusing what others have spent lifetimes trying to master. Every soul has the power to become whatever it wants to be. All it takes is the power of belief. All it takes is to have the fucking guts and balls to do so. My self-doubt gets the better of me at times. I will never lie about having a good or bad day. I will never sugarcoat my feelings and emotions to make sure I do not hurt someone else's feelings. I am too old to worry about it at this point.

I am considerate though when it comes to sensitive issues and talking points. At times, I still feel as though I am being judged when I am not. Living in my head is a frightening place to wander around. You will need company to exit safely. I often feel alone and without assurances of it ever changing. I know I have humans in my life who care and love me. I know it is never as bad as I make it out to be. The main issue is getting from point A to point Z without tripping over my own doubts and fears. My body shuts down at the end of the day. I am not worthless by any means, but I do tend to switch off my mind for as long as I can. You can only be at full gas for so long until you hit empty before you know you are depleted of all energy. It's why I do all I can with my writing before that time of the day comes and slaps the smile off my face. I saw a woman today walking her cat outside. I believe that to be the first time I have ever witnessed such a thing. I was walking around the track and it caught my attention. she was on the other side of the park, in the road, and the cat was without a leash. It was taking in everything it could before the owner told it to come closer to where she was. I have seen videos of humans walking their cats with leashes in the mountains and in all sort of places, but never in person have I seen it. The birds were flying a bit higher and I was laughing at how many times that damn cat stopped on the asphalt. It was already close to one hundred degrees with a heat index. I am sure its paws weren't familiar with such heat beneath them. It just goes to show you never know what you will see when you open your eyes a bit wider to see beyond where you are walking. This summer has been brutal. By far the hottest one on record for this part of Texas. There still has not been any rain to speak of either, which is making everything begin to transform into the brownish side of death. The only plus is the mosquitoes have been absent, which this time last year, they were everywhere, and some of them were as big as my thumb. Tailing off the end of the month, August is approaching with better chances for precipitation. Football is right around the corner as well. My favorite sport will be back before my birthday rolls around and it is always the best gift to open up towards the end of that month. Life is better once you understand how lucky we are to be here, to be underneath billions of stars, in a galaxy amongst an infinite amount of space. We forget how small we are and how minuscule our issues are at the end of the day. It doesn't take away our problems or subtract from them, but if we were able to concentrate on the positive side of being alive, we wouldn't fear as many things as we do. NASA put out a handful of images a few days ago. They were the furthest into space we have ever been able to look at. It intensified and magnified how greatly we underestimate actual life itself. I am a moon person, a sunset person, a morning person. I love all things that give my life more meaning and purpose.   Being able to see it all as I do now, I know how much I actually fucked up my life in the past for not being able to see through all of my trauma. It was probably too easy drinking as much as I was to hide and mask my pain. Nothing about growing up in a broken home is easy, nor should you be able to have hindsight until the events occur. Being the age I am now, I fully comply to my own needs now. I am entirely invested in my life. I'm dedicated to this cause of making a life I'll be able to look back on one day and be proud to tell others, I made it. I did this. What a fucking victory that will be. Even now, it's still a victory knowing I got here to bask in my success when I feel as though I am succumbing to the dark parts of who I am. A defined definition of being human is one who suffers for the sake of suffering. We all fall victim to our own wounds at some point. Though we also hold the power to come back from them stronger, bolder, and more energized prior to it happening to us. I hope you find your voice to never break for the things you love. I hope you never feel as lonely as your mind makes you out to be. If there's anything I can tell you,   it's this, once we find our meaning, everything else falls where it needs to in order to unearth and grow what we have been without. There will be setbacks all throughout life. Today is the twenty-sixth of October. I actually finished this book a few weeks ago, but decided to add another page at the end of it to compare where I am not to where I was when I started. It is still a heavy season. It is still a grieving season for me. I currently got hacked on my Facebook writing page, as well as my personal page.   I lost over a decade worth of memories and photos I'll probably never get back and over eight years of writings and work I thankfully saved or put into books. It still fucking hurts all the same. We do what we love and create all we can only for it to be taken away by someone who is trying to get into our lives by breaking into it. I don't know if I will ever understand the larger reasoning behind it. I am blindly trusting it happening for the sake of a greater change needed in my life. I never took any of this for granted. I never thought of social media as the real world by any means, but parts of it held a fond place for me. A place I could look back on memories of what I have done with my life the last decade plus. I won't ever get that back and I am coming to terms with it. Sometimes, humanity can go fuck itself, or at least those whose prime reason for existing is to inflict damage and hurt as many as they can by any means necessary. This will be the last book of the year for me. I already have an idea for the next one, which I will be beginning in January of 2023. This has been a beautiful experience to write in this form, this freeing sense of listening to the soul instead of other distractions. Two months until another year.

Chapter X

-POETRY-

one day, before the sun passes away, i'll turn to you and ask you how did i do when it came to showing you what your love meant o me. you turned me into kind eyes and clear skies when storms were killing me. life became easier once these scars were shown love, instead of being discarded as if we were not enough. you spoke to the soul i am as if you knew heaven all too well. i understood one could not speak that way unless they also knew a certain kind of hell. you still have fire in your eyes, but you loved the devil out of mine.

maybe one day i will be able to hold you as if it's all we both need and nothing more. until that day comes, a dreamer keeps dreaming of being in your dreams. you've had me since the beginning. before souls knew of bodies, before the embodiment of your eyes reflecting everything holy and set on fire. i hope these arms get around you to feel what breathing is like when it comes from a place inside of someone who replaces your doubts with certainty of a different kind of smile. you are the breaking i needed for this fever during these seasons of shakes.

the heart is the hardest part to love
when the arches collapse and become
park benches for momentary lapses
with gaps between what matters most
and what is lost. we forget the cost of
life when we went from being stabbed
to the one now holding all the knives.
a skyline is pointless without pointing
out what used to be called courageous
for loving what you knew would
become loveless and weary. hear me
now, bear with me as the ramblin'
keeps me busy and forgetful when it
comes to regret due to you.

you've always had a way with the moon, with anything worth giving your love to. you're rolling over for a few more minutes of sleep after you've turned off your alarm more than twice. you're half-dressed, a pair of mismatched socks, and a robe, just as the sun taps on your window to show you what beauty it has in   store for you. you're barefoot on a beach you've walked a hundred times before. they can try and take the mermaid out of the woman, by they will never take the sea away from your shores. i used to know your love as if it were my own. some things may leave us, but they always come back to us in another form. you can try to love her and meet her where she's at, but you will never take the running out of her. you were the best parts of me, and now, i am looking for them under every sunset that looks like you

before your alarm goes off i could've
loved you for a moon's life through
the dying light. i know not all of us
are looking to find someone else, but
i was. i still am. you've had quite a
few names others have called you by.
none of them were ever, mine. you'll
never belong to anyone despite love
being back in your life. you're a
sunday with a view, a beauty with
hands unafraid of death and the
scars it leaves behind. you were a
lover like no other, a woman with
spine and a tongue that never coward
to anyone. holding you, i knew what
a soul was. now without you, i know
what losing your heart can do.
red tips and brown eyes, things that'll
drive any dream of mine to the edge
of where hello and goodbye keep me
in-between you and everything else
that's left me.

i write about love as if i am one of the lucky few who has some of it near me to use, but it hasn't lived here in years. no one is here in this empty house, empty room, empty bed. of all the voices in my head, yours is still the one i find comfort in. all of the vices left in my life, you are the only one that feels right. the only one that takes the dark parts away from my light. you can call me a liar if you'd like. i'll even help you out when your voice breaks over the lie. but this one time, i loved you and you loved, i.

how do i look away now that i've seen the stars, the moon, and you? they tell me nothing is as good as the moment you first have together. they must have forgotten what a broken heart is capable of when life finally removes its foot from your neck to give you room to move again, to find the deepest breath you've ever fucking took in. i am always hoping you're hoping to find a way to love as if there is nothing more than us in this world.

all i need is a few open looks upon the water's edge, and the reflection will be a past i've lost, a present where i do not belong, and a future where poetry keeps a love alive and nothing more. tell me secrets as deep as the river goes. wash me in the life it has carried for miles and years at a time. speak to me in smiles, for it is the absent language of my youth that's been buried too soon. there are humans who will walk with you. there are others who will say nothing and stand beside you. i wish to be none of these. i wish to fall from vines of dead bones hanging from the stars above. i am lost, but goddamn does it feel good to not belong to anything but a kind breeze and silence upon the water's floating heart.

to know the mighty, you must know the kind of power it takes to bring down the moon each night. you must know how far broken wings must go to feel the sun. not everyone will see you. not everyone will understand you. it takes a thousand lives to live one good one, one worthy of having your name kissed by the stars as they go in search of helping you find who you are. there is no glory without tasting defeat at least once. there is no victory to be found   if you do not find yourself in the fire at least a handful of times during a war you are unsure of winning. it takes a certain human, a one in a million kind of breath to go in search of a life they may never find. but what is adventure, if you're not losing your senses and gaining a wild back in return. you are the way, the color of roses mixed with moons. you will make it. your soul is home to every universe calling out to you.

my honesty is barely given these days if i am not in solitude. i always feel eyes on me, a judgment of humanity. i wish there was a way to feel unchained, unbridled to a feeling. you are the life of all living creatures, of all light before day. may you never need restoration. may you never know this kind of exhaustion. i do not pray anymore, but i know whatever god there is, blesses you daily by continuing to give you breaths as soft as Pennsylvania snow and California rain.

you're still standing in the doorway, half-dressed and nervous. you'd think there was something lost and out of place. your beauty should never be hidden. i cannot imagine how long it took you to trust again, to think you are ready for love. a true sign of bravery is knowing when to run, when to let go. When before, you stood silent and apprehensive to all the damage staying was doing to you. i have seen birds take flight during hurricanes and wildfires. i know what is inside of you, is burning for new earth to touch, new sunsets to soak in. i know you have tried your best, and now, you get to roam as freely as buffaloes and wolves do during a harvest moon in Montana. we always get a choice when it comes to what is best for us versus what others shame us into doing for them.

some things you never get over. some things you never get through. life was made for glory, for the unending torture of, "almost" and "maybe." i wish you could've told me. i wish you knew me now. you're gone and i am left still holding onto a millions shadows all dressed as you, that all look like you, talk like you, and feel like you. you would think it brought comfort to me, but attempting to get involved with someone else will always feel as though you are near me, telling me to not let you go. cursed or tortured, i am the one in hell, while you are living your best life by an ocean that i cannot cross or ever belong to, because he is there.

i awoke with a sunrise burning through the clouds. colors like this cannot be found everywhere. you have to escape the common places, the normalcy of it all. you have to travel well beyond the rigors and onslaught of an every day life. i am not sure what i am looking for. i do not know if it is a woman or something just beyond the outstretched hand of freedom. i am trying my best to save what i can, myself included. until the next part of my journey is discovered, i will risk anything for a feeling. i will risk anything for a better chance at tomorrow.

i wish i could tell you it gets better. maybe it will. it will only cost you this life you are living, this journey of uncertainty you are on. maybe when we are older it will all make sense as to why we must suffer so much during the early stages of youth, before suffering becomes unwarranted. i want to believe the best has yet to happen, has yet to found me. i want to believe you will be there when i ask what is left for me to run to.

i have been neglecting my own life for a while now. for some reason, i never gave up believing you would come back to me. but i know now i have been the author of every scar on this heart that once belonged to you. how foolish of me to care for someone who was already being loved. i never thought i deserved anyone to begin with. i guess that's what happens when you are born with a giver's soul. you go a lifetime without letting go of anything making you feel appreciated, however briefly they stay.

i wish i could take all your pain away. the kind you don't talk about, because you never want to give someone your own problems. you are like a wedding dress at a funeral, a bit too much love itself for the dead amongst the living you try and save. it is something that's a part of you, like a child's hand wrapped around a kite's string, hoping you can make it fly again, even with holes decorating it. love to you was a precious promise, an unmasked robbery where money was never stolen. where no one was hurt. where all you asked for was a heart for a heart. you never saw the flash. you never heard the gun go off. your innocence was shot in the chest long before you were ready. i can see you now, dancing in an evening dress, while i am undressing you. love me more than death does. love me beyond the devil's grasp. i don't do promises, but i will make you one. i will make you the moon if you remain in these arms of mine.

you weren't the easiest to understand, because of how deeply you felt. it took you years to know who you were, and that is why you struggle accepting someone else's love. growing up, you were more moon than what was around you. your fascination with cosmic things have always made you more open to the world outside of your own and closed off to certain humans. being who you are is not for everyone. it is why your rarity is that of royalty. you not only speak things into existence, you are where all of the light comes from. a soft nature lives within you. a place where even the weakest of birds fly with golden wings. if all i had was one last breath to give, i would use it by telling you, thank you. not for my own benefit, but for those who know how much courage it takes living a life where giving up was an option you never took. bravery wears a smile and has a wild heart like yours. you are the reason why love has a name.

everyone i have wanted to be with turned out to be with someone else or married. every other time they have chosen to be with another. my luck in finding love has been absent to say the least. my blindness towards love itself has led me to the darkest parts of my life. i do not know if i need to change something about me in order for it to stay and stick around. the truth is, one cannot change the way a heart feels, thinks, and speaks once it is committed to the inevitable surrender when you find what you are looking for. the collapse is almost a serenity within the wholeness of discovery. there is nothing wrong about me in my eyes. i know i could probably be less of an empath, less of a worrier, less of something   else, but changing my needs, changes my identity. i cannot give up those things. i will not sacrifice more to end up with less than i fucking deserve.

love will always feel like an early morning, full of birds singing and their wings keeping hearts safe and in place amongst their actions. i hope this life becomes a thousand suns for you. i hope this life shows you a thousand moons, set out to shine its truthful light upon your journey. may you never lose your wild. may your bravery be the blood. may the light always find you wherever you find darkness competing for your attention. you are the break in my voice, and i know you will be the words when all of me is healed. my readiness has always been because of you. it will never not be you.

i never knew how far my writing could take me.   i've been grateful for it all. i could've never imagined how many others out there were suffering with an insufferable ache made from those who told us they loved who we were, that they loved us, wholly. the truth is, no one will ever love you as much as the love you give out. it might be impossible to find a true representation of it, an immaculate reciprocal. i have found it once in my life. she is gone now, but the love we shared has created new books, new life, a new beginning to my story even if i didn't want the ending to be a chapter ever included in anything i ever did with her. love is merciless, a king's denial of power when asked about a throne he sits upon. there will be a tempered reaction when it comes to love, but let it linger.

you're the only woman i've ever let hold me as you did. both arms around my body, squeezing softly just to feel me breathing. it was the first time i actually allowed myself to feel another breathe against me. i wasn't one for closeness growing up. my mother never showed it when it was needed and my father wasn't around for him to tell me what it meant. i was raised with tough love, waking up to screaming and slamming doors. i tried to love myself, but even i wasn't enough. being held became a stranger i never wanted to know better than my own solitude. i did everything possible to make sure i sabotaged any part of me anyone would ever want. i drank to keep others away if i am being honest. the meth and cocaine came in later to fend off those who were left. the pills made me forget who i was, and even then, i remembered what others had done. you see, i could never escape this place, this feeling, this unnerving possibility of becoming someone that could be loved, because someone else saw i never fucking cared about anything except loss.

you changed it all for me. when you held me, you held the child i was, the boy who grew up too quickly to take care of his brother and become an adult at eleven. you held the teenager who fucked up everything just to be different. you held a twenty-something year old who cut his wrists to leave behind what he couldn't fix. you held a lifeless body in a bathtub, waiting to die, waiting for someone to care about a life he tried blacking out every night to forget. you held a wounded man, a broken home, and all his unsalvageable parts. you made me feel what no one before you ever did. it is why letting go is impossible. it is why the sky holds onto the moon with such conviction and promise. we may be whole individually, but finding someone who makes you feel   as though you are larger than life itself, that's a love no one understands except those who've fought to stay alive after failing to say goodbye on their terms. you turned all of my pain and death i carried into poetry to keep you alive forever, to remain above the grave.

Chapter XI

-Closing Time-

There a lot of things I have shared and things I have kept safely at my side, out of anyone's reach. It isn't because I am afraid of sharing. I don't want to overshare in one book. I would rather make a series of these books and bring more of who I am to each one. But this one is about the scar on my heart and the empty part of my soul. It is about the love I have given out and the love never returned to me equally. I have found love, been in love, almost died in love, literally. There is no safety when it comes to poetry. There is no comfort zone you can escape to make yourself feel protected by its grace. There is blood, guts, gore, and anything living and crawling up from its grave. I used to live my life as though it was the only one I would ever get. I still do. I mean I lived my life setting everything on fire to watch it burn to have a story to tell later that evening.

I never gave much thought about anything else besides surviving. I've been in survival mode my entire life. It is how I am wired. It is how I breathe in a shallow sense of complacency which leads to procrastination taking over what I should have finished yesterday. It is how I cope with my life, in a solitude room with enough space for my words to find a piece of paper to rest on while my mind searches for the rest of the sentence to pair it with. When I was in love and with you, almost four years now it's been since we shared lunch that afternoon, I was all in. I had never been more devoted to anyone, ever. To this day, I still listen to Bruce Springsteen because it not only reminds me of you, it is one of the last things that connects me to you. I forget what you look like sometimes, then you will send a random picture to me. I forget what you sound like, then you will call me out of the blue. On those days I am the happiest, but after it is gone, you are gone, too. I do not know if you do it out of missing me or you get off on it somehow. Your happiness has always been at the forefront of who we were, and maybe that is where I fucked myself. It is who I had been my entire life, a people pleaser, a caretaker. Not so much of a pushover, but your love pushed me over several mountains and I laughed on the way down, as if I enjoyed it. In the definition of enjoyment, I did. I knew you were happy with what we had. I knew you were okay with the distance we shared each day and night. There was something comforting about just having you on the other end of the phone. It was one of the few times in my life I actually allowed my heart and mind to coexist together in the same space. They got along fine before you, but when I tell you all of me fell for you, I mean every goddamn bone in my body took on the shape of a smile, curving from side to side to make sure it touched both the sun and moon. I am here again, living with my father, in the same house when we first started talking. In the same bed where we spent a million early mornings talking until one of us threw in the towel for the night. Nothing but reminders exist here of the life I had with you. Maybe that is why my anxiety is still present. The comfort you once gave me is now a tidal wave and drowning me and pulling me beneath what everything used to be. I will always love you like this. I knew when we started it was going to be you or no one else. You told me the same. Now you are engaged to him and I am engaged to my poetry once more.

I guess it was a fair trade after-all. Maybe one day you'll run away to see if I will chase you. Before you think I won't, I will. Today is Sunday. My father is in the living room watching golf. There is laundry going to get us ready for the next week ahead. Summer is still scorching this part of this world. There are sinkholes forming in the front and back yard, but not the ones that will eat your house or pet. These will only break your ankle or leg if you forget it is there. Days like these remind of me being young again, wondering about what life would be like when I am older. I'm not sure when the "older" part of the thought becomes unnecessary, because it is the only thing given to us on a daily basis. As the seconds pass before us, a grayness is introduced to our younger selves that will in-turn, greet us when we are ready for age to set us apart.

I read something this morning in regards to writing and what we should be writing. When it comes to down to it, it is nothing more than exposing who you are to the world. It is sitting down with yourself each day and deciding whether or not you want to be someone who exists or doesn't. The quote I read was about selling out for the sake of being known, for the possibility of making wealth know you better. I honestly believe I never have. I may have at one point, but it was for a woman. I wrote for her, and with that, a lot of my writings were a reflection of her in the "she" form. I do not believe selling out is defined as what I did, but if it were the case, I have no issues calling myself out on it. If we only had the balls to say what we meant and how we felt. if we only had the guts to spill to distinguish ourselves from anyone else attempting to do something we were born to do. I do my best not to judge others in any way. I know how fucking difficult my life has been. I know all of my trials and tribulations are not the same as those who have lived a full life on their own terms. I do however know when I read something whether or not it is genuine or fabricated in a way to sell something he or she doesn't believe in. The world we live in now, it is all about what have you done for me lately. It is all about selling something to someone else, be it a dream, a prophecy, a quick fix, words that aren't anything more than gibberish. Pretending to be some higher form of intellect doesn't serve you well when your soul is fucking sold to the highest bidder. The only people I know genuinely, are those who are barely getting by day to day, emotionally or literally. They are the ones I connect with the most, because I have never known wealth or security in that sense. I probably have cheated myself to achieving some form of it, but I have no regrets when it comes to this path I have chosen for myself. Yes, I live at home with my father. Yes, I do not have someone to love. Yes, I do not have any friends to speak of. But at least I am doing what I love. At least I have family who supports and allows me to be myself. Growing up wasn't always the easiest thing to do for me. Always feeling different. Always trying to be yourself and express yourself in all the ways you knew how. I was never actually taught much from my parents. I learned a lot of what I know by observing and keeping still. I learned it through error and mistakes. I learned it by paying attention to details. My gifts wouldn't be what they are today without common knowledge of how to participate with yourself on a daily basis. Understanding who you are and what your joy is, is paramount. We cannot cut out our hearts or cut off our heads in order to feel something more or less. There is however a price we pay for every little thing we do. It all adds up in the end. Karma keeps her receipts. All of them. I trust it will even itself out with those who are missing payments. It took me half my life to accept the empath I was and to fully engage with that part of me. My emotions have been my greatest strength for me. They have separated me from those who are too bullish or timid to unfold them for those in their lives. I could be walking down the most crowded of streets and see something that will catch my attention. I will immediately wither, break down, laugh, smile, or entertain it as long as I am in the moment of its happening. Afterwards, it will follow me home and I will have more writings because of it. It is a welcomed guest in my house. I do not ask it for anything, but I do ask if it will help me enclose a poignant writing about what I saw. These sketches are all throughout my soul. When I refer to them as sketches, I simply mean images I see in my head of what it is I am trying to explain or set free from my thoughts. It remains a busy place upstairs, with butlers and maids all tidying up what needs to be cleaned and organized. There is a police station, a fire house, and even a psych-ward beyond the pines and over the lake no one dares to cross, but I do. I will trudge through muck and filth to get there to visit as many as I can. To get back to what I said prior before all of this, selling out isn't in my nature. Authenticity over anything else is how I approach all things. Do we hide behind who we wish we could be, absolutely. Do we hide behind those we love, afraid they will turn around one day and see we could never stand in front of them, without question. We can only do so much with what we are given, with who we have become. My life is a story many will never know, and I am perfectly okay with it being that way. Those who know, are the ones who I trust with a every one of my lives I have lived. What I do is my life. It is what I live. It is my emotional details which have given me what I have now. Knowing not to hold back when it came to anything. Moderation is a fool's game, but one that must be played accordingly. My sobriety is my religion. It is where everything pours out of me. I have planted dying suns I have seen. I have planted dead moons who got too full and overfed on their misgivings. We are all walking our version of a lonely road, an unpaved street-rally where dust and blood get you to the finish line. I began writing this book the day I was born. I knew one day I would be ready to turn it into a a voice, a face, a mirrored entity felt by anyone who looked at it. I stopped fearing the devil the day I figured out we are all walking amongst each other as one. I don't fear death necessarily, but I am aware of its power and hold it has on those who aren't familiar with it. My mindset is as positive as I can make it on a daily basis. Depression is a motherfucker, as is its twin, anxiety. They go hand in hand wherever they travel. I remember my first therapy session in 2010. My dad was able to get me in to see someone he knew close to where we lived. At that time I was still trying to fight to get my benefits back the Marine Corps took away from me when they discharged with an OTH(other than honorable). It wasn't one of those shrinks who wanted you to lay down on some red lounge couch and just spout off at the mouth to make an hour go by to get a couple hundred bucks. He was precise, caring, understanding. He was meticulous, planned, and diverse in emotional languages. If my memory serves me correctly, he had also served in the military at some point. As soon as we began the session, I felt my eyes darting all over the room. I felt my heartbeat pick up and dance around in my chest. I felt sweat beading on my brow. I felt my hands shake and me trying to keep every part of my body still. He wasn't pressing me for answers to any of his questions. He was trying to gauge my level of stress and awareness of it all. Each session was around thirty minutes to an hour. I went there for six months until he discharged me after finding out what he needed and him believing I was good to go. He had told me I was one of the most severe of his cases when I first started in regards to my anxiety and PTSD. I wasn't diagnosed with anything in the Marines. They didn't and still don't want you to mention it while you are in that you   may be suffering from it. It is a secret you keep until you get out, or at least when I was in they did. You can get one hundred percent disability if you are severe enough with it and you basically retire because of it. When I left the first session, I actually felt understood heard, and seen. I had been judged hardcore the last year or so before the initial meeting. I was still drinking at a madman's pace. I was still trying to sort out my life after the Corps. I was so fucking lost it hurt most days to get up and out of bed. I was as broken as they come back then. I was worse than a goddamn toddler I am sure. I know I gave my dad the worst experience more times than not when I moved back in with him after getting out. being labeled crazy or deranged was something I was proud of back in the day. Balance and maturity is knowing who you are despite the labels. It is not allowing it to impact you either way. I am proud of who I am today. My path is not yours. My life has never been a place for others to step foot in if they weren't allowing me to grow in some way. My purpose wasn't something I stumbled upon. It was a survival tool, a required act of defying any other outcome life had planned for me. Our lives are all different, and I hope our personalities are never questioned. The psychosis of manipulation begins at a young age. We are told one thing then showed another. Somewhere along the way we are redirected to giving up who we are to fit a status-quo, a society unkempt for change. Most of us walk in footprints already made prior to us showing up, but are made to believe it was a personal choice. I don't do well being told what to do. I learned what kind of animal lives within me the day I understood grief, death, and being unloved as a young kid. My quietness is only there for your protection. My shyness is only there for you to see who I can be when I am not disturbed. Never allow anyone or give someone the power to destroy your soul. A lot of us do it well enough on our own and do not need another to assist in it. We are born with blood on our hands. The act of life is trying not to get any of it on anyone else. It has been years since I began sharing my words publicly. I wasn't sure I could or wanted to. Back in 2014, I was outside on the deck of our house. I saw the water reflecting on the ocean and it all came back to me gently with love and acceptance. The conviction. The urgency. The truth. The promise I made to myself as a kid to find what made me happy and not who made me happy. I began again that day and never looked back. Today is Friday. There is still no rain to speak of and my first time writing in this book in over a week. I took some time off to get some other things done. I do not need to write every day. It isn't really a choice I have. My mind isn't always locked in on certain days when I feel the energy is off. Last night was the Sturgeon moon. I had been feeling her relentlessness all week and even before then. We are such moonly creatures. The water inside of us trying to find its way home while moving us as it goes. The tug and pull of her light. The ebb and flow of her power. it is a miraculous sensation I believe we all take for granted. Being alive is such a painful experience for a lot of us. It begins when we are young, and as we grow older, the pain seems to mature and grow alongside us. I hope to have this book out sometime in November. By the rate I am going, I will have it done a few months before then. I want to give each page its own space and room to breathe. It is how I would want to be treated if I were it. My life has been heading towards a path of more solitude as of late. Some days it is hard for me to make sense of it all, but I do my best with the language of my soul by honoring it, by accepting I won't always have days when I want to create. It is the way of the artist. Recharging and retreating back into your own shadow for a bit to recoup and recover what you have given to the day or week or month. Though we are creatures of habit, we must break loose of it once we are too familiar with ourselves as we currently are. If we are not striving to dig deeper into our psyche and inner workings, we are failing ourselves and those who helped us along the way to get to this point. Wherever you are in your life, I hope you never stop searching for a grander meaning of why. I hope you never give up the chase to pursue something beyond your control. We are only here for a few extra breaths, a few more than those who left us too soon. I do not want you to waste it nor do I want to waste any of my life contemplating what could have been if I had done this or that. My life revolves around my writing, my sobriety, and my mental health. All three are the only children I have. I will fight with everything I have to protect them at all costs from those who try and interfere with my progression towards being a better version of myself. The most precious part of life, is believing in yourself during a time when no one else seems to be capable of it. Some of us are thrown from the wreckage before it ever comes into contact with said object. Love demands us to believe in everything we do, even if we are unsure of the outcome. It is one of the most difficult things we can do with our lives. When giving into love, we give into something greater than ourselves. We give into the temptation of serenity and fate crossing over into a human form for us to invest in. Becoming who we are meant to be, involves tragedies along the way. Oftentimes they are human names, faces, a feeling unrequited. We meet them and we understand more about who we are and become less infatuated with any other part about living. Some times it can last years, decades, an entire lifetime. But for some of us, the healers, the helpers, the creatives, we are left to be alone and discarded. We may not have what they need, but we are the happiest of them all, because our purpose goes beyond love itself. It is a calling not everyone will ever feel or understand. You can talk about it until you are blue in the face, but no one will get it unless they know what it is like to be one of those. We are alone for a large part of our lives. We choose our art over anything else because it has saved us. It has loved us back unconditionally. It never asks anything more than we already give to it. The relationship we have with our gifts precedes anything anyone ever has tried to put in front of us. The happiness lingers like a wilderness seeking less shelter. There isn't much left we haven't either felt or done. The curators of our own cause. The lanterns of our own light. Hope itself visits us daily. A motherly figure of Mary and all of the angels find their way towards us. I am not a religious human, but having an out of body experience will turn you into a believer of magic if anything else does. My free spirit will not be tied down by what society thinks I should do or needs to do. I have never been one for rules. I was born a rebel as soon as I found out my mother drank too much. She did it to cope, to survive as crazy as that sounds. Being on the drink turns you into someone you are not. Every face has a double we are unfamiliar with until life takes us into a direction we have yet to go just to see the expression it can make and leave on us. When we are ready to see it, we are made aware of its presence in our lives. I have given myself away a few times too many in recent years, though I have yet to find anyone who could keep me the way I needed. I do not believe I will ever settle down. I thought I had found someone who could give me more, but she ended up giving it to someone else without telling me until she was ready to break my world apart, after telling me she never would. The dark days found me then. The sun died and went away to join its moon on the other side where her darkness could be appreciated and adored. Love doesn't ask much from us. All it needs is to be seen, to be known. there have been days when everything I touched, I felt its pain. The magnitude was never lost on me how every living thing has a soul, how every living thing knows of loss. It is crucial we pay attention to the light inside of it all. I know this book won't be a best seller. I know it will be only read by those who have supported me from the beginning. I know there isn't money to be made in this industry unless you sell your soul or have found a niche to be a part of. All of my words are truth and honesty. It's why readers are trepid to pick up my pages, because they will be able to feel the agony within. They know it will open up old wounds and scars they had left dormant, afraid of awakening them. If I am being honest, I rarely read anything these days. If it isn't something from a dead poet or song lyrics from a favorite artist of mine, I don't give it any attention. Nothing alive these days gives me an emotion strong enough to pursue it. It's a sad thing some would say, but they don't know what it's like picking up on the energy around you and compartmentalizing it your entire life. My escape lives within the pursuit. My escape becomes an outlet for those who wish to be here and support my work. Over the last three years my Instagram and Facebook pages have died. I have lost well over fifty thousand followers because of their algorithms. I have lost money because of it. I don't and have never done this for monetary gain or fame. I honestly couldn't care less if this book sells or doesn't. Those who have read and still read my work, is more than enough to get me beyond the dream and into a reality where I have all I need. A writer's life is nothing more than a starvation of sorts, where the only thing being fed are the pages themselves. The one thing it gives back in return is a fullness only achieved if you are fucking brave enough to shed your insecurities and be prepared to feel seen for the soul you are, for the truth you are pouring out to be consumed by those with minds willing to sift through it. Today there was thunder crackling as the birds flew through. There were dogs barking, because they needed something more than an empty backyard to run around in. My stomach lay empty, deprived and aiming for something more than whatever scraps I have left to eat. Everything is starving these days. Nothing gets feed on time. Someone is always late. Someone is always holding back. Writing this book has shown me more of who I am and more of what I am capable of if I sit down long enough to appreciate this longing I still have for you, instead of crumpling it up and throwing it away outside of my window for the wind to pick up.

I'm the sum of all the parts my mother kept running from. I'm the sum of all the parts my father could never teach me. Loss is my mistress. Grief is my outwardly approach to living. Distance is what I carry with me when someone believes they can love me. My family has been a backbone and my sad face all at once. I am not sure how to love if I'm not losing something in the end. I remain wounded and sheltered from the beating I had endured after you left. Some days I want to do nothing more than suffer alone, in peace, without distraction. It's the only way for the art needing to come out of me to be honest and trusting. I am my mother's son, all twisted up with a convulsing rage. There's still love here for you, but this life is no life without you. You left me while you were loving me. Your lies became these scars I write about. This place is where the lonely go to die, never to be seen again. My hope rests with the moon. These will be the last pages ever consisting of you and the torture you put me through. This will be the last book that will ever give you shelter and keep you from the life of me. These are all of my truths being aired out and dried for safe keeping should someone stumble in while I am folding them neatly to put away. There is a place I go at night when I feel my eyes begin to tear up from all of the emotional stress I feel. It is a softly said word, in-between my fingers and hands where I feel someone hold me in that spot. I feel a comfort, a tightly knitted promise for my dreams to wear. I am closer today to who I need to be than I was yesterday. I am closer to finally riding you of my life once and for all. You will be married when this book comes out. I wish you nothing but the best, but I know my best would have been more than you ever knew. But I'm happy things didn't work out. I'm thankful you are there now. It means I saved myself again from dying for someone who never would've lived for me. I have loved or have been involved with three women over the last ten years. All are either married, engaged, pregnant, or have a child. I do not hate, love. I hate how high I placed it amongst my priorities. I hate how much power I gave it in my life. Being in a broken home, all you want is comfort and adoration in some type of form. All you want is consistency and a place to rest your worries, knowing whatever comes the next morning won't be there to try and harm you in any way. But love is love, and I will go down to the abyss with it. One day, I will have my happy ending. More soul than human, I remain for love, for war, for poetry.

<u>YOUR SPACE</u>
<u>A place for your feelings.</u>

I wanted to dedicate at least three weeks of journal space for you. It can take that long to truly know yourself, to know who you are trying to become, and to change anything about your life that needs to be removed or added. I hope you find closure within your own words. I hope there is enough space for you to feel free, to feel as though you are making the steps needed for the journey at hand. It doesn't matter how much you write or when. The only thing that matters is you fucking start somewhere. Make your own story. This is what I want for you. This is my own way of saying, thank you. Writing doesn't come easy for a lot of us. Sometimes there is simply too much to say to even know where to begin. This is your sign to start. It doesn't have to make sense. It just needs to be let go of. I hope these blank pages will give you courage to follow through until the end and start another journal, and then another one. I hope once you start, you never stop letting it all out. You'll be amazed at what you're capable of once you know how to breathe easier by giving the pages everything weighing you down. May this become a catalyst for the artist in you, for the human you've always been but never had anyone to tell you in person. We are not what we think. We are not what others say. We are what we do with the life given to us. May you never view failure as being the end of a lesson. Life is about mending every broken light. It is about restoring anything anyone has ever broken inside you, so that you can love yourself again if needed. Infinite love and blessings to you.

SONDER   4 3 3

SONDER   4 3 3

SONDER   4 3 4

SONDER 435

SONDER 435

SONDER 436

SONDER 436

SONDER 4 3 7

SONDER 4 3 8

SONDER 4 3 9

SONDER 440

SONDER 440

SONDER 4 4 1

SONDER 4 4 1

SONDER 4 4 3

SONDER 4 4 3

SONDER   4 4 5

SONDER   4 4 5

SONDER   4 4 6

SONDER   4 4 7

SONDER   4 4 7

SONDER 4 4 9

SONDER 4 5 1

SONDER 4 5 1

Psychologists suggest it takes 21 days to break a habit. I strongly believe in this. Some take less. Others take more. if you put your mind to it, you will be able to render down who you were and change everything you want about your life. Being a recovering alcoholic, each day is my best day. I make it a point to write about it at least once a day. If you made it this far with the book and have used the empty spaces for a journal, you will read this. I am proud of you. I know we are all hurting. I know there is so much unknown in the world today. Everyone is struggling and we should be able to talk openly about it. No one needs to or should be suffering alone. I hope you were able to journal the way you needed to and in a sincere way that by the end of it, your soul felt lighter and your light felt brighter. We are all after something we may never hold. It is the beauty and the cursed way of life. Each of us may have something to prove to someone else. Each one of us has been told we were worthless in some form or another. I am here to tell you, I see you. I appreciate you taking the time to put in the work necessary for you to either move on or inject more of yourself in this life you are a part of. This universe needs you. Your purpose may not have been found yet, but I know there are humans out there who have benefited greatly from knowing you. SONDER is such an honest way of looking at life. We are all our own story living within other stories we know nothing about. We are the main character in our own story and an extra in someone else's. I imagine photos of random people making up the rest of the faces and knowing someone out there knew them and loved them. You are loved, dearly.

9 7 9 8 2 1 8 0 9 7 2 7 1